LIVING
HUNGRY
IN
AMERICA

Other books by the authors

J. LARRY BROWN:

Hunger in America: The Growing Epidemic

H. F. PIZER:

The AIDS Fact Book (with Kenneth H. Mayer)
Coping with a Miscarriage (with Christine O'Brien Palinski)

LIVING HUNGRY IN AMERICA

J. Larry Brown & H. F. Pizer

Foreword by Victor W. Sidel, M.D.

Macmillan Publishing Company
New York

Macmillan Publishing Company
866 Third Avenue, New York, N.Y. 10022
Collier Macmillan Canada, Inc.

Library of Congress Cataloging-in-Publication Data
Brown, J. Larry (James Larry), 1941–
    Living hungry in America.
    Includes index.
    1. Food relief—United States—Case studies.
2. Poor—United States—Case studies. I. Pizer,
Hank. II. Title.
HV696.F6B76 1987   363.8′83′0973   87-5496
ISBN 0-02-517290-5

Macmillan books are available at special discounts for bulk purchases
for sales promotions, premiums, fund-raising, or educational use.
For details, contact:

Special Sales Director
Macmillan Publishing Company
866 Third Avenue
New York, N.Y. 10022

10 9 8 7 6 5 4 3 2 1

Designed by Jack Meserole

Printed in the United States of America

To Kelli and Alex, for whom I
  seek a better world,
And to Judi, who is an example of
  what it can be like.
And, for Chris and Katie.

CONTENTS

FOREWORD

This book describes a scourge upon a bountiful land, an affliction that was totally preventable. It is a tale of human suffering and political intrigue, the story of a modern-day epidemic caused by political ideology and negligent leadership. It is a journey across the United States to places few of us ever see.

On the evening of February 25, 1985, the national television networks reported that some twenty million Americans were hungry and that the problem was getting worse. Veteran NBC commentator John Chancellor, obviously moved by the extent of hunger, warned that "the veneer of civilization seems to have worn very thin."

On a May evening one year later, the President of the United States took to the television screen to defend his administration against criticism that government was doing too little to stem the growing tide of hunger. Hungry people, Mr. Reagan asserted, were simply too ignorant to know where to get food.

The group that documented the extent of hunger in 1985—a team of prominent physicians assembled from around the nation—was the target of the President's criticism a year later. In one of the most compelling accounts I have ever read, Dr. J. Larry Brown and co-author H. F. Pizer take us into the halls of Congress and the meeting halls of small-town America. We go to the doors of the White House and behind the doors of poor Mississippi tenant farmers. We experience with the doctors the painful sight of babies dying in their first days of life, and the frustration of trying to convince political leaders to respond to the tragedy.

We experience the emotions of Brown, who becomes a familiar face on national television only later to become the target of political attacks and a death threat. We go with him and his colleagues to visit the most powerful leaders of our country, where they plead the case for those who have no power to plead for themselves.

We learn details about hunger in America and, ultimately, much about ourselves as a people. We see how compassion gets swept aside by political ideology and how some of our most serious diseases are caused by people. Above all, perhaps, we learn that we *can* do better and are inspired by the authors' conviction that hunger in the United States is one problem we can solve relatively quickly—given the political will to do so.

That this latter point is true seems hardly beyond dispute, especially since the U.S. nearly accomplished this goal once before. In 1969, President Nixon convened a White House conference on hunger, attended by some 3,600 people; the recommendations this group submitted to Congress reflected a bipartisan consensus that hunger has no place in an affluent democratic society. The actions that followed, under the leadership of both Republican and Democratic administrations, were based on that consensus and were demonstrably effective.

But the consensus was short-lived. Little more than a decade later widespread hunger was to reappear in America. It returned quickly and grew rapidly, its ravages proving lethal to many of its victims and to the spirit of the nation. As hungry babies succumb to preventable disease or death, a part of each of us dies as well.

This story reveals how utterly ludicrous is the existence of hunger in America. We read in disbelief that in Chicago there is a soup kitchen run by Missionary nuns who have come from Calcutta to feed hungry Americans. The spectacle of volunteers from India coming to feed people in this wealthy nation somehow sears the mind.

Within the past few years, some twenty studies have pointed to an epidemic of hunger in the United States. In 1982, the U.S. Conference of Mayors reported that hunger was a "most serious emergency." Their bipartisan plea for help was preceded by a Department of Agriculture study that found that hunger "is increasing at a frenetic pace."

During the next two years, the Salvation Army, the National Council of Churches, the General Accounting Office, and many other organizations sounded similar alarms. To these were added a multitude of state studies that found hunger quickly spreading. Remarkable in their consistency, the reports cut a large swath across the nation: there was hunger in California, Florida, Maryland, New Jersey, Ohio, Oklahoma, Oregon, Texas, and Virginia, among other states.

In New York, my colleagues and I at the Montefiore Medical Center and Albert Einstein College of Medicine organized a "Hunger Watch" project, which both confirmed and exceeded our fears. Despite heroic efforts, churches and social service agencies have been simply overwhelmed by the mounting tide of hungry people, many of them families with young children.

While all research findings were pointing to a massive problem, government officials in Washington tried to minimize its magnitude. A top presidential aide dismissed hunger as "anecdotal." One or two cases are anecdotes, but when they appear in every state, rising rapidly in numbers, those cases constitute an epidemic.

We would know a great deal more about hunger and its health consequences had not some political leaders limited data collection by federal agencies. Almost as if to ensure that citizens did not learn the facts, the administration used the reins of government to curtail analysis of policies.

My colleague, Dr. David Rush, led a group of distinguished researchers in analyzing the supplemental feeding program for poor women, infants, and children (WIC). Every year the administration has tried to cut WIC funds, but Democrats and Republicans in Congress protect it because of its effectiveness in producing healthier babies.

Yet when Dr. Rush's group reported their findings to the Department of Agriculture, which commissioned the study, the administration withheld the results for nearly a year. When they were released, positive findings had been altered and minor criticisms of the program had been highlighted. These changes were made not by professional staff but by political appointees. This incident seems to typify the political lens through which some of our government leaders view hunger. Instead of seeing suffering that requires a response, they worry about political implications. Sometimes they try to silence the messengers.

During the years in which this story unfolds, the doctors from the Task Force were attacked by politicians for "being political." Senator Jesse Helms of North Carolina charged that they were traveling across the nation because it was an election year; two years later the doctors were labeled "ivory tower eggheads" for not traveling more.

Obviously, the critics cannot have it both ways. But those who seek to deny the magnitude of hunger in the U.S. are not logical. Their concern is not to find the best information about hunger in America, but to discredit those who report it. We might smile at their inconsistencies were the consequences not so serious. For as this story reveals, behind statistics are the tears of children and the frail bodies of the elderly. When ideologues obscure their misery, problems remain and people continue to suffer.

Helms and his bedfellows are but a parody of something greatly wrong in our nation. Our decency as a people seems to be smothered under a blanket of political maneuvering. Some would rather "win" than do what is right.

Since the beginning of this decade, fundamental changes in policy have taken place that produced a sharp increase in poverty. As millions more Americans fell into economic despair, others benefitted at their expense. Today the disparity between rich and poor in America is greater than at any time since official figures were first kept by the Census Bureau in the 1940s. "Robin Hood in reverse" has become a sad reality.

In my travels as President of the American Public Health Association, I frequently was asked whether we have the resources to eliminate hunger in our nation. We do. Other industrialized countries with more limited resources have done so; obviously, we can, too.

The problem is not our resources but our priorities. In recent years we have witnessed the most massive military build-up in the history of the world. We went from spending under $160 billion on arms in 1981 to nearly $300 billion in 1987. The expenditures amounted to $1.6 trillion in just seven years, or $12,000 for every taxpayer in America. If we had spent a million dollars a day since the birth of Christ, the total expenditure would have been only half that for the weapons outlays of the past seven years.

This is money that did not go to feed pregnant mothers or to nourish small babies. It is money that could have prevented disease among the elderly or provided work for the victims of plant closings. It is money that could have made small farmers productive or built houses for the homeless. In short, as President Eisenhower warned us some time ago, every dollar spent on the military is a robbery from the national treasury—extracted from the quality of life and opportunity for our people.

This book is about an America under a mischarted course. *Living Hungry in America* is about the suffering that has resulted from that error, suffering that has occurred just as surely as if it had been spread by a contagious disease.

But this is also a book about hope—not the fanciful hope

of dreamers, but the hardheaded hope of realists who have exposed the politics that cause hunger and point to a higher road to be traveled.

—VICTOR W. SIDEL, M.D.
Distinguished University Professor of Social Medicine
Montefiore Medical Center/Albert Einstein College
of Medicine
President, American Public Health Association, 1984–85
President, Physicians for Social Responsibility, 1987–88

PREFACE

This book is the fulfillment of a promise I made reluctantly, about an odyssey I never really planned.

On the beautiful island of Martha's Vineyard, off the coast of Massachusetts, I begin to recall the millions of families who know no such luxury. Indeed, many of them must go without the bare necessities of life. I know because I have seen them, and I can never forget them.

The images remain vivid in my mind: nine-year-old Lee, whom I discovered in southern Missouri, a child so malnourished that he looked to be three years younger; Mrs. Chavez in the valley of Texas, a loving mother who had but three tortillas for her children's dinner the evening of our visit; Matthew, the middle-aged victim of a plant closing, who took his family each day to a local soup kitchen; and Effie, an eighty-nine-year-old woman who told us she doesn't feel hungry as long as she doesn't think about food. They remind me of the thousands of others whose names I have now forgotten—fathers driven from their homes by welfare restrictions that deny help to intact families, working mothers cut from the food stamp program because of a five-dollar increase in monthly income, handicapped people told that they are no longer disabled and so denied food stamp and other federal-program assistance.

These are American citizens. Their pain is too great to be ignored; their plight too common to be dismissed. They are visible to anyone who looks. They can easily be found in every state of the Union.

For three years I led a national team of physicians into the homes of Americans who are poor and hungry. Reserved and usually reticent, they answered our questions and suffered our intrusions. None of them ever asked us for anything, but I resolved that I would tell the story of these people. I believe that if the dimensions of their suffering become widely known, the American people will act to end a preventable tragedy.

I am a member of the faculty of the Harvard School of Public Health. Starting in the spring of 1983, however, my usual work was relegated to second place as evidence of a dramatic increase in domestic hunger began to demand more attention from myself and my colleagues. Staff from the Project Bread Hunger Hotline had come to Harvard to ask for help in responding to the growing number of Boston families running out of food each month. As director of the School's community health program, I recruited faculty and students to help this small organization establish a system to monitor food distribution among 207 emergency food centers in the area.

What we learned alarmed us. The number of people relying on handouts to keep from starving was far higher than had been reported in the most audacious press accounts. But this was just our introduction to hunger in America. Our response to a simple request would ultimately consume the next several years of my life and much of the time of a diverse group of doctors from around the nation. Many of us would never be the same again. How it all happened and what we learned is part of the story I want to tell.

Professional people, especially in the fields of health and medicine, often work alone. But occasionally events impel us to move outside the usual channels, into new areas and new ways of working. That is what happened in this case.

The real beginning came after I consulted with Dr. Julius Richmond, the former Surgeon General of the United States and a colleague at Harvard. Upon hearing of the unexpected size of the hunger problem in Boston, Richmond turned to the subject for which he is best known: babies and children. He knew that area doctors had begun to see and report an increase in the number of cases of malnutrition among youngsters from poor families and that they traced much of it to a simple lack of food at home. We decided to convene a meeting of faculty, staff, and policy analysts to determine what might be done to address this problem.

After two days of deliberation we agreed that initial information on hunger and illness was somewhat alarming, but that more data would have to be obtained on a systematic basis. I then asked a group of physicians, scientists, and religious leaders to join us in investigating the extent of hunger in New England. Several local philanthropic foundations provided modest support for travel and office supplies.

During the last months of 1983, we left the staff to carry on research activities at the university and we traveled by car to each of the six states in the region. We broke up into small teams to search out hungry people in each state and to talk with them and the community leaders who try to help them. Altogether some twenty-eight doctors participated in this unusual quest.

We traveled the back roads of rural Vermont and the highways connecting the old mill towns of Western Massachusetts. We went to New Haven, Connecticut, home of Yale University and the seventh poorest city in America; from there we traveled to Providence and Warwick, Rhode Island. We held a public hearing in the capitol of New Hampshire and went into the small towns of Maine, arriving along with the first snowfall of the season.

What we found was highly disturbing. There was widespread hunger everywhere we went. When we reported our findings, others shared our dismay. Finally the nation was shocked when the *CBS Evening News* reported on our discoveries.

I was then asked to mobilize a national team of physicians to see whether the situation was unique to New England, or whether America was experiencing a silent epidemic of hunger. From across the nation some of the more prominent names in American medicine joined me in this new effort. Deans of medical schools and schools of nutrition and public health, chairs of departments and pediatric programs, a surgeon and the Surgeon General, practicing clinicians and some now retired, eminent researchers and hospital administrators, all came togther in response to this problem.

The two years that followed were an extraordinary, intense adventure. We were to enter the private lives of ordinary people and become aware of the inordinate power of leaders who affect their well-being. We were often made joyful by the decency of common people and angry at the policies that caused them so much pain. We laughed at the antics of little children and were moved by the tortured lives they led. We would know the extremes of depression and determination, fierce resolve and intense exasperation. We would become the subjects of highly positive press attention and of greatly personalized vilification. I found myself speaking on numerous national news programs. I testified before Congressional committees as to what we had seen, and I was able to plead for those unable to plead for themselves.

But as much as I enjoyed feeling professionally useful and personally fulfilled, I was greatly saddened by the darker side of the America I had seen.

Anonymous hate mail, expressing utter contempt for the poor, arrived. Political extremists disrupted my speaking engagements. High-level Washington officials tried to get me fired from the faculty of Harvard University. I even received a telephoned death threat from a citizen of Montana.

None of this, however, disconcerting as it was, made us

consider stopping. It was all mixed in with our efforts to determine the causes and consequences of hunger in the world's wealthiest nation, and end its ravages upon our people.

We traveled to nineteen states and the District of Columbia, often staying for a week at a time. In each state the eight or ten colleagues who had joined me would be augmented by that many more local physicians who had agreed to help. Teams of doctors, accompanied by other health professionals, social workers, and clergy, would fan out across the state, covering rural areas as well as cities. We visited hospitals and clinics to talk with medical colleagues and their patients. We inspected schools and day-care centers. We rode vans that take food to the elderly, and forded country streams to reach isolated families. Most of all, we visited homes, thousands of homes, asking people what they had eaten before we arrived, and what they would have after we left. We looked into refrigerators and pantries, into the empty faces of adults and children with empty stomachs. We saw anecdotes turn into facts, and vignettes into reality.

This is the story of what we saw and what we learned: It is the flesh and blood behind the statistics; the story of a growing and totally unnecessary tragedy. The story of living hungry in America.

—J. LARRY BROWN

Martha's Vineyard, Massachusetts
August 1986

ACKNOWLEDGMENTS

We express our gratitude to the many people whose lives and work made it possible for us to tell this story.

In our travels across America, we met literally thousands of people who promote social justice. They are the people who run emergency food programs in church basements, the health professionals who look beyond illness to the conditions that cause it, the public officials who truly are public servants. They believe that our nation can do better, and they work toward that end.

We pay tribute to the physicians who left busy schedules to crisscross the nation in search of the hungry, and to the members of the news media who accompanied us because an important story needed to be told.

We are grateful to Dean Harvey Fineberg and other colleagues at Harvard who believed in this undertaking and to the Field Foundation and USA for Africa, as well as numerous smaller foundations that made it possible to carry out our mission. Special appreciation is due staff members who arranged busy schedules and frequently bore the brunt of hateful letters and threatening calls: Debby Allen, Judy dePontbriand, John Kellogg, and Glenn Wasek. We thank our agent, Jerome Agel, and our editor at Macmillan, Alexia Dorszynski, for their guidance in bringing this work to fruition; and Dick and Maud Williams for their assistance.

We thank photographer Steve Haines and the *Providence*

Journal for supplying photographs that capture the essence of what we describe in the text.

Finally, and above all, we are grateful to the poor of America who permitted us to come into their homes to learn of their story.

A NOTE TO READERS

It may be a bit unusual to encounter a first-person account by two authors. As head of the team of physicians that traveled across America, J. Larry Brown chronicled his and his colleagues' experiences. To Brown's narrative, H. F. Pizer added material from the field notes of the other doctors. Their collaboration produced this unique story.

LIVING
HUNGRY
IN
AMERICA

1

Winter in New England

THE VOLKSWAGEN BUS glided across the icy highway as I tugged at the wheel to regain control. The possibility of landing in a frozen ditch on the way to New Haven was a terrifying beginning for myself and my colleagues, a group composed largely of physicians from the New England states. We had been scheduled to arrive in New Haven at 8:00 A.M. on this cold December morning, but the road conditions would make that impossible.

This was our first field investigation into hunger, and we did not yet know what to expect or whether our efforts would prove to be beneficial. Some of the group were doctors who had medical practices in clinics and hospitals. Others were ministers from churches in the region. Yet, others were academicians from medical schools and public-health institutions. We had, however, two things in common: most of us were quite inexperienced in what we were doing, and we all were determined to see how bad hunger really was and why it was a problem.

In New Haven several physicians and two ministers joined us, establishing a pattern of involving local professional people wherever we went. Altogether our group numbered twelve people, which allowed us to divide into three working teams for greater efficiency. Over the next month, we were scheduled to take teams into all six New England states. Starting in Connecticut had been a random choice.

One would not think of Connecticut as a state in which hunger would be found. It is second in the nation in per-capita income; its suburban towns have brick homes with well-kept gardens, and the more rural areas boast sprawling farms with stone fences. Its major cities are headquarters for big blue- and white-collar industries, particularly insurance. But Connecticut is also a state of contrasts. Alongside the wealth is poverty, often extreme poverty. Hartford is the fourth-poorest city in the nation, and New Haven, home of Yale University, is the seventh-poorest.

We had come to look for the poor and the hungry. Our group split up into smaller numbers to visit homes and agencies in the community.

THE DOCTOR TREMBLED WHILE EXAMINING THE CHILD

We pulled up outside the tenement exterior of Christian Community Action, a social service agency on Davenport Street in one of New Haven's more residential areas. Run by Reverend Karl Hilgert, the agency had recently been in the news. On a rainy winter morning only several weeks earlier more than three hundred people had lined up at seven-thirty in the morning to get surplus government cheese.

"Little did we anticipate the response," Hilgert said. "All those people standing in the freezing rain for two hours before we opened."

Active in city-wide efforts to feed the hungry, Hilgert shared his disappointment that demand so far outstripped need. "During the past three years, more and more soup kitchens have opened, but the food is not sufficient for the increasing numbers of people who come." Hilgert called the hunger in the city "simply staggering."

Hilgert took me to a decrepit apartment that is part of the Christian Community Action building. "They are homeless," he said, pointing to a mother and three children. I could see the family was happy to have the warm shelter, even if its torn wallpaper and dark interior seemed depressing to those of us who were visitors. Out of work for more than a year, Linda Tyson received inadequate assistance to feed herself and the children.

Pediatrician Debbie Frank asked the mother what she had been feeding the baby. "She's ten months now, and the doctor says I should be starting her on cereal and strained vegetables. But I can't afford all that, so I just nurse her."

We later learned that Linda's attempt to stretch the food for her two other children was not always a success. We also learned that her situation was not that uncommon. At a nearby day-care program for children under the age of three, the administrator told us that "the majority of our babies come here hungry. We give mid-morning snacks right when they arrive because they are lethargic. They wolf them down and begin to perk up." She mentioned that she and her staff go into the homes of children and frequently find that they have nothing to eat. "The cupboards are bare. The refrigerators have no milk," she added.

At the Christopher Columbus Elementary School later that day I heard the same story used to describe life for older New Haven children. Principal Haywood Thaxton showed us around the school where he tried to meet the needs of children for whom he is responsible. "A lot of them come to school hungry. . . . Many of them are tired and listless," he noted. Thaxton found a special irony in the fact that the first words some of the youngest children learn to read are those on the school menus.

Debbie and I left to join other doctors at the nearby Fairhaven Soup Kitchen, an emergency feeding program attached to a local health center. Several hundred people were there for a warm meal. Debbie has a way with children and immediately hit it off with a child she estimated to be about three years of age. For most people, judging a child's age is guesswork, but not for Debbie, who is a developmental specialist. I have observed her in clinical situations at Boston City Hospital where she can correctly estimate children's ages within a month or two.

But this time she had guessed wrong; the mother said her daughter was six. Thinking the mother had misunderstood her somehow, Debbie asked the child's age again and got the same response. Now incredulous, Debbie asked the child to open her mouth, knowing that the number of teeth would confirm her age. Her professional demeanor could hardly conceal the shock: the little girl was indeed six, but virtually all the teeth in her mouth were rotten. Bending over the little girl, Debbie's hands trembled as she tried to zip the child's jacket. "What does she eat?" she asked the mother. "We don't have much in the house. We eat mostly what we get here at lunch. Sometimes I give her sugar water for the calories."

A few days later the little girl was written up in a feature story in *The New York Times*. Reporter Dudley Clindenon had observed Debbie's examination of the child and the discussion with the mother and had used the encounter to capture the general situation we were to see that day. I was pleased that an independent source had been along to confirm the devastating impact hunger was having on children in the state.

The man who runs the Connecticut Food Bank sees hundreds of hungry children. "A quarter of the people served in soup kitchens in the state are kids under the age of ten," reported Mark Patton. Another quarter, he said, are teenagers. As if to underscore the seriousness of the problem, Patton asked questions that required no answers: "Whatever happened to that exclusive male club known as the soup kitchen? Why is it that half the people fed nowadays are children?"

Patton was hasty to add that while his special concern is children, elderly people who are poor fare little better. "Many of the elderly have pets who eat better than they do," he said, citing the example of one woman he saw recently living on Wonder Bread, government cheese, and Tang, while her cat ate tinned cat food.

During the course of our day we visited with unemployed people, primarily former breadwinners and their families. Forty-one-year-old Agnes Burgon of Danielson had been raising five children since losing her husband several years ago. All of them, she said, were big eaters in the age-range of ten to seventeen. "By the third week of the month, I'm praying I have enough money to make it until my food stamps come on the first." She described the monthly scenario in which first her food stamps, then the supplies in her pantry give out. She dips into rent and utility funds to give the children at least one meal a day. This practice increases her indebtedness, which, in turn, means that she must later dip into her food budget to pay her bills.

We would soon find Agnes' story repeated throughout the New England states and, later, in our travels across America. Families must choose between heating the house or buying food, between groceries and medical care, between utility bills and milk. Their choices seem impossible.

"THERE'S NOTHING LEFT"

That evening we attended a public hearing at the Unitarian Church on the Green. Directly across the street from the campus of Yale University, this did not seem like a place to discuss hunger, but people had come from around the state, some of them professionals concerned about the hungry they try to assist, some of them ordinary people suffering the daily fate of being hungry themselves.

One of the more moving speakers was Dr. Stuart Wolfe, director of maternal and child health for the city of Hartford. A soft-spoken man, Stuart somberly talked about babies born in that city. "One in fifty will die before reaching the age of one," he said. "No group of people has been more impacted by federal budget cuts than women and infant children. We see a country where the quality of each child's life is not really cherished."

Reverend Alvan Johnson had driven to New Haven to tell us that of the five hundred people in his parish, many go hungry. "I cannot feed them alone; I need some help from the federal government. Elderly people are paying utility bills and going without food to eat," he said.

At first I wondered if any hungry people would be willing to speak up. Twice I invited them to share their observations with us, acknowledging how difficult it might be for them to do so. I told them that the group of physicians assembled before them was used to seeing human need and that we all wanted to understand their own problems better. Finally, a woman came forward.

Jacqueline Putnam paused and then said, "I live on a dead-end street. It's in a small town called Sterling. I know six families that are desperate." At first I thought she was a social services worker or church representative; but something told me to pay close attention as Jacqueline spoke with real anger about Washington officials who think everybody in need is a cheat. "All they have to do is get off their rear ends and go out to the towns and see for themselves. Come to my street; I'll show them the people."

Then she began to talk about her own situation. "We're a middle-class family. I have four boys. My husband is hospitalized. We got no money and our food stamps last about two weeks each month. My sons are all in their teens, growing boys. The school serves no hot lunches and no breakfast. We

have no car. The nearest soup kitchen is fourteen miles away."
By now the words were pouring out, steadily and quietly.
Her eyes began to fill with tears. "The last food I bought was
yesterday. I spent the money my fourteen-year-old made
shoveling snow. There's nothing left." I could not bring myself
to ask her any more questions. The answer had already been
given. She had nothing left.

Sybil Nassau, who coordinates the Meals-on-Wheels program in Hartford, had waited until the families could speak
about their circumstances. She then told about the elderly
she sees in their homes. Of 358 households interviewed by
her staff, one-fourth had no food available on weekends when
the meals were not delivered. "That's none. Zero," Sybil
stressed, as if to let the number sink in. "Elderly people are
willing to work to get food to eat, but many are trapped in
their homes by illnesses or handicaps. Recently I tried to get
one seventy-two-year-old to go for the government cheese
distribution. She looked at me and asked, 'How can I stand
in line to get cheese when I can't stand at the sink to wash
my own face?' "

Doctors and nurses treating these old people frequently
report that they are anemic. They need more food but it is
not available. "We often place meals in entirely empty refrigerators," Sybil explained. "I wish you could see the man
who weighs eighty-five pounds and lives on coffee and hot
water, or the old woman who had to call the Red Cross for
food, or the people who hear of federal budget cuts and are
scared to death that they will lose their only meal of the day."

Following the public meeting I dropped my colleagues
off at their hotel; I would meet them at five-thirty the next
morning to leave for Rhode Island. I spent the evening with
a friend, Burgess Carr of Liberia, who served with me on the
board of Oxfam America, an international relief and development organization. I told him what I had seen during the
day, and he and his wife were aghast, saying that my words
seemed like a report from a poor African nation.

"IS THERE HUNGER IN RHODE ISLAND?"

The next morning we dispatched five of our doctors by car to Newport, Rhode Island, where they would visit surrounding communities before joining us that evening in Providence. Their itinerary included a visit with the Narragansett Indian Tribal Senior Citizens' Council, stops at a food distribution center in West Greenwich, and discussions with the medical staff at the Warwick Health Center. Altogether, their day was packed with eight stops along the way, and I felt somewhat guilty about expecting too much from them after the stress of the previous day.

My team drove directly to Providence, arriving at the Calvary Baptist Church for a nine o'clock briefing by Mike Morrill, director of the Rhode Island Food Bank, on the hunger situation in the nation's smallest state. "Is there hunger in Rhode Island?" Mike said rhetorically. "I need only five minutes of your time. In Providence four bread lines serve over one thousand people a week. One morning last October people stood in line over an hour for a stale loaf of bread. That's hunger and seeing it will convince you."

It was now December, and we had come to take him up on his offer. A short time later we were at the John Hope Settlement House, where a line of people waited for a loaf of day-old bread and pastries. Arriving a bit late, we pushed past the cameras and reporters from the local television station and went directly inside to talk to people who had been standing in the raw chill.

I could see that the recipients and staff were startled by the sudden appearance of well-dressed doctors and the glow of television lights. Fortunately, Gordon Harper, a Harvard psychiatrist and veteran of previous field investigations, was quick to recognize their uneasiness and moved to chat with some of the recipients. The friendly small talk worked, and we were soon involved in conversation.

I met Dave Ferguson, a twenty-six-year-old father with a small child in his arms. Dave was bewildered by my approach until I told him who we were and why we had come. The man opened up as I talked with him, but I learned a lesson that I would remember in subsequent visits to other states around the country. Dave had come to get food for his baby, nothing more. He had not come to whine or complain to anyone. He had most certainly not come to tell his story to some Harvard professor and his friends while television cameras loomed in his face.

Slowly and quietly, Dave told me his story. Out of work for six weeks, he had no money. His wife lay ill at home, and they could get no medical care because they had no insurance. I asked him what his little girl had to eat. "This," he said, gesturing to two pieces of biscuit wrapped in a napkin. Bewildered as to how the infant could consume a biscuit, I pushed him to explain. "I roll up little pieces of bread and soak it in water so she can swallow it. Then I put it in her mouth."

Later I related the experience to Mike Morrill, reminding him that he had said people wait in line to get bread. He had not said that some of them try to keep their babies alive on that bread. Morrill's Food Bank distributed a million pounds of food the first year it opened. Two years later, at the time we visited, it was distributing three million pounds, and still it was not enough. "Our distribution reflects what we are able to do, not what the need is," Mike emphasized. He referred to the people at the small agencies that distribute the food his bank dispenses as "dike-holders." We met a number of them at other agencies that day.

Asata Tygrai watched as we spoke with hungry people in a line at another emergency food center. "It looks like the lines of people you see trying to get food in Poland," observed the staff worker. "On most distribution days at least two hundred people stand in line, old people and parents with young children, to get bread that is one or two days old."

At the Olney Street Baptist Church, Reverend Michael

Turner's program was stretched to the limit. "We see hungry people begin to line up at three-thirty on winter days for a meal that won't be served 'til five. They walk two to three miles to get here and wait for over an hour to eat what we can give them. Blacks, whites, adults, children. . . . It's ecumenical suffering we see here."

While we were visiting Providence, our colleagues were finding similar circumstances in other communities in the state. In Newport, for example, community leaders reported that without the emergency feeding programs, the weekends would be "fast days" for many families in the area.

Debbie Frank later reported what she had seen in a soup kitchen: "I met two teenage girls who were clearly scavenging for two tiny girls ages seven and five. They'd watch the serving window for an extra corn muffin or juice, then urge on the younger ones. They told me, 'Sometimes we sneak the food home, but we have to hide it in our coat.' "

The town had a soup kitchen run exclusively for children. It started when staff at a recreation center learned that many of the youth had no dinner each night. Asked why there were cinder blocks on the floor in front of the serving window, a counselor explained that many of the clients are children too small to reach the food without assistance.

Patricia Abbate coordinates food programs in the nearby Warwick area and told our visiting team that "in the relatively middle-class communities the number of those in need of emergency food has increased dramatically." Church leaders in that area as well as Pawtucket and East Greenwich shared statistics on the food pantries and soup kitchens they operate. There, as at Reverend Turner's in Providence, need was substantially outstripping demand.

Later in the day our team reconnoitered at Mike Morrill's food bank, located in a nondescript warehouse on a seamy side of Providence. We were ushered into the huge steel facility through a freight door, finding it dark but warm inside. The staff had hot coffee ready for us to drink while we inspected their operation and talked with religious and social services representatives from the area who had volunteered to answer our questions.

Only minutes after we had entered the warehouse and scattered among the boxes stacked on pallets across the floor, I heard someone calling me. Looking up, I saw Dudly Clindenon beckoning to me. "Dr. Brown, would you look at these boxes?" he said, pointing to the cartons piled two and three high all around us. Seeing that I had missed his point, he continued, "Don't you see, this is all junk."

On each of the boxes was stenciled its contents. Scanning the containers, I read "pickles," "marshmallows," "cake mix," "instant potatoes," and "Jell-O." I had gotten his point by this time and hurried to explain food bank operations.

Food bank people are the first to say that they run a mop-up operation. They take food from wholesale and retail grocers and food manufacturers, food that is out of date, old, or somehow undesirable. The donating firm gets rid of unwanted items and takes a tax write-off for doing so. The food bank salvages what it can and donates the food to churches and other organizations that feed the hungry. The food is usually of good quality because the operators take great pains to see that it is not rotten.

Still the reporter was correct. Most food bank items, while safe to eat, are nutritional junk. Junk that corporations donate in order to take a tax write-off.

Morrill and the others assembled at our impromptu warehouse meeting gave us a startling picture of the people who get the donated food. One vivid in my memory is the woman who drives a school bus in the area. Her husband is terminally ill, dying of cancer, and she supports the family on an annual salary of $8,700. Her children often go to school with no food in their stomachs, but they do get an evening meal—from what their mother is able to get at a food pantry.

Joining this family is the former real-estate appraiser who was laid off from his firm. Having exhausted his unemployment insurance, he is now losing his home as well. He worries about where his wife and three children will live. Meanwhile they eat food contributed through the food bank. So, too, does the fifty-nine-year-old engineer who is too young to receive social security but considered too old for another position. The company for which he had worked over thirty years had left the area, leaving him no pension and no termination benefits. He eats once a day at a soup kitchen.

We finished our day with visits to the Capitol Hill and Alan Barry Health Centers, where we met our colleagues. In informal discussions with medical staff and some legal services attorneys who joined them, we learned of the increasing difficulty needy people were having in qualifying for federal nutrition programs. Attorneys and doctors alike spoke of the growing "red tape" faced by families who were out of food and going hungry. They described the people who cannot seem to qualify for food stamps even though they are penniless and the children who have been cut from the school lunch program.

Nutritionists and physicians described the health effects of the conditions they see every day: children who are anemic, babies experiencing growth failure, and elderly people who are more susceptible to chronic disease because of nutritional inadequacies. "The more we dig," a local doctor said, "the more we find. Someone comes in, saying they're not feeling well. Or a baby seems not to be developing normally. Upon examination we find physical symptoms. Then we find that the whole family is in trouble. They've got nothing to eat."

CHRISTMAS IN VERMONT AND WESTERN MASSACHUSETTS

Six days later we headed off again.

Leaving Harvard School of Public Health at 5:30 A.M. again, we took just over three hours to reach our initial destination in Vermont. The radio informed us that the temperature was eight degrees outside, a cold so bitter we could feel it even inside the bus as our toes began to hurt.

My thirteen-year-old daughter Kelli was along for the trip, sitting next to Dr. Carola Eisenberg, Dean of Students at the Harvard Medical School. A tall and gracious woman, Carola wrapped an extra jacket around her own legs and those of Kelli as they huddled in the far back seat of the bus.

When we reached the kitchen of Myrtle Birsky's Family Center in Springfield, Vermont, we found Christmas decorations in the steamed windows and several families sitting quietly at the wooden tables eating the meals the staff and volunteers served. "It's a crying shame," Myrtle declared to no one in particular. "These are proud people . . . proud but beat down. They suffer a long time before they'll show up for a meal, but they're hungry. I haven't seen it this bad since nineteen forty-one."

Myrtle Birsky is the kind of woman you think of when you hear the words "Vermont kitchen." Warm and somewhat reserved, she has lived in the area most of her life, fifty-five years. "I know these people," Myrtle assured us, "and I've seen things get a lot worse in a few years. There are people hidden away in the hills who seldom come out. They eat little because they have little. They suffer alone. They keep their pain to themselves." But they come to seek help because of their children, Myrtle went on to explain. Pride takes a back seat, at least momentarily, as entire families file in to sit down for a meal, then file out again. "Not since nineteen forty-one," Myrtle later repeated, assuming that everyone knew the year the Depression was winding down and a war beginning. "It hasn't been that bad since then."

"WE SHARED AN EGG"

In the surrounding communities we found the people Myrtle Birsky had described. Following the narrow Vermont roads back into the hills, our local guides took us into the areas we said we wanted to see. Picking out a house here and there, we piled in and out of the car during the course of the afternoon. We knocked on the doors of cozy cottages with wood smoke pouring from the chimneys, often finding refrigerators inside sparsely filled.

A young woman told us that her husband was out of work, but her part-time job as a waitress helped them and their two young children scrape by. "I fill the kids," she said, pointing to a three-year-old son playing with a plastic truck on the floor near a hot stove. "But I don't feed them well. We get food donations, you know, moldy pies. We subsist . . . I can't say we really live." In a log cottage tucked behind trees and large boulders a mother nodded when asked if her family had eaten that day. When asked what they had eaten her response was direct, "We shared an egg."

Between home visits we stopped to see Joy Morrell, who serves on the school board in Waterbury and runs the state supplemental feeding program for women, infants and children (WIC). Joy said that Vermont has the highest participation rate in the nation in the WIC program, an accomplishment of which she was justifiably proud. But it is her "other hat" that she finds disturbing. As a member of the school board, she told us, she learns from the guidance counselors that significant numbers of the children are hungry, distractible, misbehaving. "Teachers report that more and more of our children are having problems, problems which can be traced directly to not enough food in their homes."

Fanning out into small towns with names like Rupert and East Dorset, we went to find the children Joy described. We put on hiking boots and trudged through snow to cottages hidden in small clearings that could not be seen from the back roads. Accompanied by Marcia Russo of the Visiting Nurses Association, we found a 44-day-old baby in a home with no food and little heat. The infant was better off than an older sister who no longer nursed. We went with the head of the Meals-on-Wheels program to the home of an elderly man who lived on five meals a week, all of them delivered by this program. He had no income and listlessly chopped at a log to obtain splinters of wood to burn in his stove for warmth. His granddaughter would be coming home from school soon, and he wanted to be sure the fire was alive enough to warm her short visit. Her parents were hardly better off than the old man; the one thing they could share with him was their daughter.

Late that afternoon we went back to Springfield to visit the Unemployment Council located in the hall of Local 218 of the electrical union. A white-shingled building, the structure consisted of a large open room with a handful of chairs and two tables near the front. We were welcomed by Jean Cisco, who assured us that some of her members would be along soon. As we waited, Jean described life for the 900 Council members in the area, most of whom joined because they need food.

"I guess we can start now," Jean announced after getting us around the tables where some fifteen to eighteen former workers had gathered. "These are the doctors I told you would be visiting us today. I hope you will just tell them what they want to know. Don't anyone be bashful, you got nothing to blame on yourselves."

The Unemployment Council had been started in the town as a support group for unemployed people, to provide an opportunity to share woes, discuss what to do, and mainly, to learn that the common problem the people faced was beyond their individual control. Once started, however, Jean said, "Food became *the* issue. People got tired of discussing the lack of jobs and their feelings about being unemployed after years of working. They were hungry."

The people did not look hungry. Under their coats, caps, and woodcutting vests, I imagined most of them to be on the heavy side. I know enough about nutrition to realize that this meant little since hungry people often try to fill up on fattening food. My quest for visual proof gave way at the words of a middle-aged man at the end of the table. Looking at us from behind plastic-rimmed glasses, he began with moving words, "I ain't here to complain none, but I do wish something could be done for our son. He's just fifteen and we ain't got enough to keep him fed."

Robert Turner had worked for twenty-seven years, doing whatever kinds of jobs were available. He had never asked for help before, a point he stressed three times during his brief statement. In fact, he still wasn't asking for help, at least not for himself. It was his son's hunger that had prompted him to come to the hall to meet a group of strangers.

A woman who later identified herself only by her first name looked as though she might cry as Robert spoke. Once he was done, she began to talk immediately. "It's hard seeing your kids with so little to live on. It's real hard. I got two myself, one's just five. We were doing all right 'til I lost my job when he was sick. Now I can't find anything." In response to our questions, she said they were getting milk to drink; a neighbor had cows. It was food she worried about. The children were not getting enough to eat.

Some of the people were angry, although with a subdued kind of anger. They did not raise their voices, used no strong language. But they were angry about life, mainly about being helpless when they had always been self-sufficient. Their anger—the anger of people unaccustomed to desperate times—was something we would find across the country.

By eight that evening we were registered in rooms at the Hartness House in Springfield, an authentic New England inn managed by Ida Cahee. After dinner, we talked about the day's experiences. No one seemed despondent, but all of us were deeply troubled. New Englanders ourselves, we had invaded Vermont at Christmastime to find that there was hunger in the beautiful little towns—and we had found it easily. It was very disturbing.

ON THE TRASH HEAP OF AMERICA

Early the next morning we drove down Route 91 to Turner's Falls, Massachusetts. Most of us knew what was happening in the Boston area, but this was new territory. Joining our entourage for the day were two local physicians.

At the time of our visit, Massachusetts was an unlikely place to find hunger. It was enjoying the lowest unemployment rate of all major industrial states, and its economic base was strong. A system of nationally unique health clinics stretches throughout communities from the harbor of Boston to the Berkshire Mountains in the west, providing care for the state's poorest residents.

Our staff had miscalculated the distance from Vermont, a fortunate mistake which allowed us to arrive forty-five minutes before our first meeting of the day. We dispatched one carload to the meeting site; the rest of us went to visit an elementary school we had spotted upon our arrival in the town.

Turner's Falls is an old mill town, and the Sheffield Elementary School, a two-story brick structure on Crocker Street, looked as though it had been built before the town had been founded. We finally found its front entrance and proceeded directly to the office of the principal. The secretary was very helpful to three strangers who appeared unannounced while her boss was away in a classroom. When he appeared we explained why we had stopped by.

"Hunger is the magic word," the principal began. "We know there are quite a number of children in this school who do not get enough to eat. It is a matter of growing concern among my teachers." Unfortunately he was not able to let us in the classrooms to talk with teachers and students due to the unexpectedness of our visit. Almost to the front door on our way out, the principal took Ken Dean, a Baptist minister who was a veteran of the 1968 hunger field studies, by the arm. "Things are pretty bad," he whispered. "I hope you people can do something."

Later in the morning we met with Mike McPhee, who directs a Head Start program in the community. Of the eighteen children in the program, Mike told us, most are hungry. "Almost all of them are from unemployed families. The families run out of food toward the end of the month and the children get dizzy, unable to concentrate. Some eat whatever we can place in front of them."

An hour later, following the rigorous itinerary for the day, we met with a group of elderly people at a Franco-American Club. The site of a feeding program for the elderly in the town of Athol, the Club serves a hot meal every day to senior citizens in the community. We learned from the director that she is happy to offer such a needed service but is frustrated by her knowledge that many of the old people have little or nothing to eat at home. "Social security checks and pensions do not last, especially not with the cost of medicines and utilities. The old people," she continued, "always pay their bills first; then they take whatever is left for food. It usually is not enough."

We heard a similar account when we stopped by the Lithuanian Club, where a meal program is run for unemployed workers and their families. We had been invited to eat with the guests. The three long tables in the hall were packed when we arrived. Most of the diners were families. Others were couples beyond their childbearing years. Three of us entered the hall and were encouraged to stand in the serving line. Vegetables, macaroni, hot gravy over bread or potatoes, the meal might not have won a nutritional award but it was tasty and filling. With full plates, we left the line and split up to talk with the guests.

The crispness of the day was absent from the warm hall, but so, too, was the joy of the holiday season from the faces of those present. The workers were quiet for the most part, concealing a quiet anger I had found among their unemployed counterparts in Vermont. Most had worked all their lives, owned and cared for homes, generally played by the rules. When a local tool-and-die company decided to leave the state to seek greater profits elsewhere, many lost their livelihood. With the jobs went medical coverage, life insurance, a way of life. Unemployment benefits had run out. Families once middle-class were now destitute.

"I made a profit for that company for thirty-three years," Chester Davis said. "This is my reward: they close up and lock me out of my job. No job, no unemployment, no nothing. What am I going to do?" He finished speaking to look at his teenage son, who sat quietly next to him, then shifted his gaze to the remaining potatoes in his nearly empty plate.

Chester's quiet despair was drowned out by the man across from him. A bulky, middle-aged man, his anger was suddenly unleashed by the comments he had just heard. He turned in his chair to two of us and commanded our attention by telling us he had something we needed to hear. "We're proud people, the best damned toolmakers around," he began. "We helped build America. Suddenly we are screwed. Out on the trash heap. Why is this happening? Why is our government treating us like this? Why are they caving in?"

As the man spoke, his voice rose in anger and bewilderment. The questions rolled off his tongue, carrying the pent-up emotions that his new circumstances had fostered. "Something bad is happening in America," he continued. "We're the victims of a 'slash-burn' mentality. Companies come into a community, stay several decades, extract all its profits, and leave. Well, what about the families left behind? Is our government so helpless to do anything about it?"

In Washington, the General Accounting Office (GAO) had recently issued a study of people served in emergency food programs. It concluded that no longer are the recipients mainly alcoholics and mentally ill people. Today they are the "new poor," people who have helped build the nation, contributed to the economy, and supported the programs that help sustain others through hard times. Other national studies had begun to corroborate this observation. Now we were seeing the phenomenon firsthand.

During the remainder of the day we made house calls in the countryside. In the town of Orange, we visited an elderly couple whose farm no longer produces because they are too old to work the land. Inside their little white house, surrounded by fallow fields, we found a refrigerator with a loaf of white bread and a stick of butter.

"What did you eat last night?" one of the doctors inquired.

"Some macaroni and a chicken leg," the wife responded.

"How about today, what have you had?"

"Nothing," she answered.

In a nearby community we stopped at several homes where young children were present. One family was joyous over the father's recently acquired job and reported that they were well-fed. As the mother talked, she added that her little boy seemed to be doing well now. Not long before a physician had found her son to be anemic. The residents of another home had no job over which to be pleased. Charlene McNeil was worried about feeding her family for the next week. A look in her refrigerator revealed some vegetables and cheese, enough for the time being. It was the next week, when her food stamps would run out, that worried her. The previous month her family had gone several days without food.

The hunger we saw in the homes we visited in Western Massachusetts unquestionably was part of a statewide pattern. The Salvation Army reported steep increases in the number of people seeking help. More families than single people were in need. Father Ed Tinsley, a priest who helped start a food bank in Worcester, described the need as "constantly escalating." In fact, the three food banks that operate in the state distributed 1,680,000 pounds of food during their first year of operation—over 800 tons of discarded produce and other items. The next year the number jumped to 3,200,000 pounds.

"We feel like the National Guard," confided Nan Johnson of the Boston Food Bank, "only we don't have the trucks."

The National Guard analogy may be appropriate. If the 3,200,000 pounds of food were placed on National Guard trucks in the standard eight-to-a-mile convoy, it would fill up the Massachusetts Turnpike from Boston in the east to Springfield in the west—a distance of eighty miles. Yet the analogy is misleading. The food is never enough because the need for it is continuous. Unlike a natural disaster when the need is greatest for a few days until things return to normal, hunger in the state goes on, day in and day out.

Normal for some is the situation described by Suzanne Buglione, a young worker at the Pernet Health Center in Central Massachusetts. She recalled taking rice and bread to a mother who had called in desperation. "When I arrived with rice and five loaves of bread, the mother met me at the door and revealed that they had not eaten in forty-eight hours. She took the food from me and gave it to the five children. To my astonishment they tore open the bags of bread and consumed every piece of it in less than thirty minutes."

Hunger is also the normal state of affairs for many patients discovered by Massachusetts physicians. It is a normal day-in, day-out state of affairs. "My patients are poor and elderly," says Dr. Emilio Carrillo of the Harvard Medical School, who runs a clinic in Cambridge. "Many have chronic diseases and should be on special diets. How can I take care of a seventy-eight-year-old widow with arthritis when she can't afford decent food and lives on Rice Krispies for six months? No medical care can make up for the physical harm she suffers or the degradation she feels."

RURAL MAINE AND NEW HAMPSHIRE

We had only one week to prepare for our next trip, a foray into the small towns and back roads of rural Maine, and from there to New Hampshire. During this time we received a surprise telephone call from the staff of Charles Kuralt at *CBS News*, asking if he could accompany us into the field. For years I had watched this veteran newsman give his travelogue reports from around America, closing with the familiar words, "This is Charles Kuralt, on the road." We were delighted that Kuralt's years of experience might serve to help the nation better understand the problem we were uncovering.

It seemed as though we had picked the worst possible month in which to travel. We had had an ice storm on the way to Connecticut, bitter cold the week of our trip to Vermont. Not to be outmatched, Maine provided a heavy, icy snowfall as we made our way along Route 95 toward Portland. Earlier we had sent a team of doctors to Augusta and Bangor to the north, where they would meet the Governor and several small-town mayors, and make home visits before joining us the next day.

Daphne Blackburn, an internist at Cambridge Hospital, and Jeff Burack from the Harvard Medical School were on this trip. In Portland we were to meet two other physicians who were making their way there independently: David Halperin, a surgeon who practices medicine in Maine, and Deborah Prothrow-Stith of the Boston University School of Medicine.

We left Harvard at six that morning to allow ample time for our first meeting three hours later. This time my ten-year-old son Alex accompanied me during our fieldwork. Twelve different events were planned for the day, and there would be an informal public hearing that evening.

"MOMMY, WHAT'S APPLESAUCE?"

Despite the bad weather we arrived only slightly behind schedule, and were taken by local volunteers to the basement of the People's Regional Opportunity Center. Cozy and warm, the room looked like the church basement in any small town in America. We were grateful for the good hot coffee.

The purpose of this stop was to meet the local residents who would brief us on the area, to go over our itinerary for the day, and to catch up with our colleagues. In place of Charles Kuralt, who was unable to come, we met veteran correspondent Robert Pierpoint, who told us that Kuralt still intended to do a segment on his program the following Sunday. Yet another television network had sent a crew, and local press were in attendance as well.

Sixty-year-old Frederica Wagnis, who runs a food pantry in Portland, led the briefing. A mixture of rural Maine folksiness and reserve, Freddie was one of the key people trying to respond to growing hunger in the Portland area. She told us that we would be going to little towns like South Paris, Casco, Naples and Norway, names that produced images of faraway places. "This will help to peel back the curtain of rural poverty," Freddie said, as she presented background information on the growing number of Maine residents who were falling into poverty.

We stopped first in South Paris, a quiet little town with wide streets and two-story buildings. It could easily have been the setting for a production of *Our Town*.

We met with the town manager in his corner office, with swinging gate doors separating the clerical desks from the entryway. The manager was in shirt-sleeves. He listened politely as I tried to ease his Yankee wariness by explaining why we had come to his community. Midway through my comments he pulled a file from his shelf and began leafing through pages whose corners were dog-eared from prior use.

"We're showing a pretty good increase in town spending for emergency food donations," he reported, but the statistics were hardly those which would astound an outsider. "One category of town spending went up from $3,461.70 to $5,132.40, and another we call 'emergency assistance' increased by about one hundred percent to a total of nearly $4,000." Recognizing that the numbers themselves meant little, Daphne Blackburn asked the manager to describe more generally what was happening in his community.

"What's happening here is about the same as always was happening," he began, "only now it's worse. The people here eke out a simple living, but it seems like things are getting worse instead of better." Rattling off the names of families in economic distress, the man frequently mentioned the names of children, demonstrating his knowledge of the community. But his description lacked an underlying analysis, making what he had to say interesting but not particularly insightful.

The South Paris fire station was our next destination. The firehouse doubles as a site for a feeding program that provides a daily hot meal to seniors from the community. The television cameras had preceded us.

The atmosphere almost seemed festive, the conversations reflecting the importance of the noontime meal in a community that probably has few other social events during the long Maine winter. But the people were not there for the festivity, according to director Maureen Jeffrey. "Most of these people are low-income," she told us. "For a majority, most of them, I'd say this is their only meal of the day."

Nearly seventy-seven, Esther Brummel, one of the diners, lived alone on a pension from her deceased husband's employer. "The $277 a month does not go far," she said, but seemed uninterested in talking about her situation. As I kept urging her to do so, she added, Yes, she liked the food here. No, she did not want more, even though it would be her only meal for the day.

"What if you get hungry tonight?" I inquired. "What will you do then?"

"I won't get hungry," was her response.

"But if you did?" I continued.

"I can't get hungry tonight. There's nothing to eat."

Esther had nothing in her refrigerator except the remains of an omelette, which she estimated was several days old. Yesterday she had taken home a roll from her meal at the fire station. She had consumed the roll last night with a cup of hot tea. She had some oil and flour in the pantry but nothing else that she could remember. Except for the tea bags.

"I was getting food stamps but they stopped," she informed me. "I don't know why they stopped coming."

"Mine stopped, too," chimed in Hattie, who sat next to Esther, but offered no last name. "They said I wasn't qualified anymore but I didn't do anything different." As I pressed for details I learned that her income is even less than Esther's. Her social security check had increased about four dollars a month. "That's when the lady at the office told me I couldn't get stamps any more."

Maureen Jeffrey moved me aside while Daphne continued to interview the ladies and Alex listened to their conversation. "If you go in their homes you'll see how they live," Maureen said to me. "It gets pretty depressing. Most of them have so little of anything, including food."

We made a number of home visits that afternoon to homes selected by our local guides. Ninety-one-year-old Robert Jacobs lived alone with his cat in a one-room house outside the town of Casco. Like Hattie and Esther, he had recently lost his food stamp benefits. The contents of his refrigerator did not speak well of the benefits of living on a limited income; Daphne opened the door to find a bottle of ketchup, a piece of bread still in the original blue-and-white wrapper, and half a tin of cat food. The old man's last meal had been the previous evening. Two potatoes, sliced, fried, and sprinkled with the ketchup. He would have nothing to eat that night.

"How often do you go without eating?" Daphne asked him.

"Sometimes I get several meals in a row," he responded. "Other times I don't have anything for a few days. Sometimes—I just don't really know." The old man's voice trailed off, his attention seemingly captivated by the swirling wind that blew snow against the window of his kitchen.

A short drive away the Androscoggin Home Health Service nurses told us that they were seeing a dramatic increase in hunger among their homebound patients during the past year or so. One nurse called the increase "really high," and expressed concern that there were fewer alternatives for feeding the old people. Facilities such as St. Luke's Kitchen, to which the nurses previously sent referrals, now were running short of food supplies. St. Luke's was in fact serving double the number of people it had previously, with the clientele fairly evenly divided between elderly people and families with children.

In Lewiston we stopped by the Oasis Soup Kitchen, which was having problems keeping up with increasing need. Located in the middle of a city block in a neglected side of town, the Oasis looked like a cheap café, with small tables spaced across the linoleum floor and a grill counter at the far end. It was run by a fundamentalist minister who said he would talk with us, but only if everyone agreed to keep politics out of the discussion.

"The Lord will do what is necessary," he said. I sat at a table with Rosemary, a middle-aged woman with a teenaged son and a younger daughter. The little girl had on a lightweight sweater and no coat, despite the blustery cold temperature and snow outside. Rosemary had brought the children for a meal " 'cause we don't get much to eat at home." As she talked the boy buried his face in his plate, trying to hide his self-consciousness. "Chris is the sick 'un" she added, gesturing to her daughter. "The principal said she gotta stay back if she misses any more days." The family lived on an income of $345 a month, nearly one-third of which went for a two-bedroom apartment. Heat was another $80, not leaving much for food. Dinner usually was potatoes, cooked in a variety of ways to avoid monotony.

After Rosemary and the children left, the minister said that there were a lot of poor families in the area. "It's a wonderful opportunity for churches to show their Christian love." The man resisted numbers. He didn't know how many people in the area were hungry, or how many he fed. He hated the government, too, stressing at every opportunity that charity ought to be used to feed the hungry.

"That boy of Rosemary's looked pretty embarrassed about being here," I ventured, trying to test the limits of the man's views.

"Mighta been," the minister conceded in an unflappable tone. He paused, then started up again: "Mighta been, but humility ought to be learned at an early age."

Once outside, as we walked along the sidewalk out of earshot of Alex and our local guide, Daphne said, "Those people in there clearly need the food, but I think the Reverend needs them even more." We would run into this type of charity mentality in other communities, often associated with fringe religious sects that ran emergency food facilities. Some people seem to need other people upon whom they can bestow their charity. Part of the inclination seems genuine enough: someone is hungry, so feed them. But when you press these charitable givers, you get the sense that while they would never say so directly, they need the hungry to *stay* hungry. It is merely a matter of charity, and they feel good feeding the hungry—even if it means that the hungry stay hungry. If Rosemary's son was embarrassed by having to eat in a soup kitchen, the answer was not to provide a means to enable the family to be more self-sufficient; instead the boy should learn humility.

Freddie Wagnis did not fall into this category. She had invited us to stop by the food pantry she runs in the basement of the Woodford Congregational Church in Portland. We had made our way back to the city by late afternoon and found Freddie waiting for us. Part of an interdenominational group of twenty-two churches, her program had seen an 83 percent increase in the number of families asking for help during the past two years. Cans of food neatly organized on shelves made the small room look like a basement grocery.

Freddie excused herself to chat with two women waiting to receive a two-day supply of groceries. Accepting their words of appreciation, Freddie's grandmotherly expression vanished as she returned to talk with us.

"I get a little upset when they say there's no hunger," Freddie admitted. "I see women who eat peanut butter and bread here in our hallway because they've had nothing for forty-eight hours. I see little children look at the food and ask: 'Applesauce, Mommy, what's applesauce?' "

"Is It Soup Yet?"

Our colleagues who had gone further north for the day were learning from the Governor of increasing hunger all over Maine. His observations were backed up by the data offered by Human Services Commissioner Michael Petit, who told us that local general assistance had increased by 50 percent that previous year and did not begin to meet the need. "I question the sanity of anyone who downplays the need," Petit offered. "The truth is that except for regulations which continue to hurt the poor more and more, we get no interest from the federal government to respond to human need."

If government officials could have attended the citizen forum at the Revere School, there may have been greater interest than that which Petit described. Despite the snow and the fact that the forum was held during the dinner hour, the nicely carpeted hall was almost filled to its capacity of two hundred people. Our colleagues had returned from the north to participate in the hearing; we all sat at a table in the front. After introductions and our opening comments, the Mainers began to speak as a television sound man held a boom microphone close to each speaker.

The school principal began by expressing concern over

the children in his school who were not getting enough to eat. A nurse said that more children were being diagnosed as anemic. A woman from the St. Vincent de Paul Society said the number of people coming to their soup kitchen had gone up from six thousand to nearly eleven thousand in less than a year.

Slowly, hungry people began to speak, much like their counterparts in public hearings in other states. After listening to what others said about them one or two would tell about their own circumstances. Then others found the courage to speak up. Some had tears in their eyes, like the woman who told us, "My husband stayed at home tonight out of embarrassment. Our family is hungry and he can't stand to say it in public."

Others, like the father who held a son in his arms, gave dignified statements about their conditions and their fears. Overwhelmingly, people spoke about children—their children, other people's children, children who did not get enough to eat. I thought about the little girl whose mother was unable to buy applesauce.

Our schedule the next day began at 7:30 A.M., and lasted until our departure for Boston in late afternoon. The last event was a meeting held where we had begun the day before, the basement of the People's Regional Opportunities Council. It was to be a debriefing session, where my colleagues and I would share observations based on our two days in the area. Local and national press had come to record the event, and I asked the doctors who had gone to Augusta and Bangor to report first, with my team members following. I was to summarize and thank the local people who had helped to arrange for our visit to the area.

As I spoke I noticed that several people in the audience had smiles on their faces. Since I had not said anything humorous, I turned to Alex for a clue. Facing the wall behind me, in full view of the entire audience, Alex had found a medium to vent the frustration and anger in his ten-year-old mind about what he had observed the past two days. Under a banner that read: IS IT SOUP YET?, Alex had used a magic marker to sketch pictures of President Reagan, the First Lady, a Secret Service agent, and Ed Meese on an erasable wallboard. The contorted faces and grotesque features served as Alex's own explanation of hunger in the area, the firsthand experience of a child who had come face-to-face with a problem he did not like. None of the cameramen present took advantage of the situation by recording the genuine feelings that Alex expressed in his artistic catharsis. But a local photographer did take a picture of the boy and his finished product, and that is now one of my cherished treasures.

"WE HAVE NO LEFTOVERS"

Less than a week later we again departed from the Harvard School of Public Health, this time bound for New Hampshire for the last leg of our investigations.

Socially and politically, New Hampshire is one of the more conservative states in the nation and is perhaps the antithesis of neighboring Massachusetts. Its motto, "Live Free or Die," is a throwback to colonial times and epitomizes much of the state's philosophy. New Hampshire has no state income tax, few social services, meager government spending for schools, and a decided distaste for public regulation. Lack of attention to environmental regulation threatens the state's rural beauty. Some critics of the state jokingly suggest that the motto ought to be changed to "Live Free and Die."

Central to New Hampshire's political climate is the *Manchester Union Leader*, the only paper published state-wide. Run for years by editor and publisher William Loeb, the *Union Leader* has espoused the right-wing ideology that originally prompted Loeb's support for the ultraconservative John Birch Society. Before his death several years ago, Loeb reveled in the spotlight of presidential primaries every four years, using the front page of the paper for savage editorials against candidates he did not like. On the day we arrived in the state with our delegation of doctors, the *Union Leader* ran an editorial entitled "Hunger Mongers." Although our hearing at the state capitol was organized entirely by state residents, and although several New Hampshire physicians joined us for our work there, we were attacked as "carpet-baggers." The central thrust of the editorial was that there was not really any serious hunger in the state, and that outside agitators had come to stir up an issue.

Instead of field visits to surrounding towns and communities, our work would consist of a day-long hearing at the State House where New Hampshire College students and faculty had arranged to have busloads of people from around the state come to meet with us. The hearing was organized by Dr. Ira Goldenberg. A longtime personal friend, Ira has served in various educational institutions, first as a professor at Harvard, next as president of a small college, and then as dean of a college in the city where the hearing was held. The event, with few public officials being asked to testify, reflected his way of looking at the world. Instead, businessmen, religious leaders, and social service professionals from small communities all over New Hampshire were brought before us. Mixed in throughout the day were hungry people who had been invited to attend by agency people, ministers, and through public radio announcements about our visit. We wanted to know what was happening in New Hampshire, and Ira had undertaken to fulfill that request.

As we entered the hearing room Monsignor Philip Kennedy of Manchester took me aside to point out the hostile editorial. "This is what we're up against," he confided, "and it's why your coming here is so important." Not fully comprehending the meaning of his gesture, I thanked him for the welcome and asked if he would join us at the hearing table for the course of the day. As it happened we were in a continuous hearing from 9:00 A.M. to 6:00 P.M., during which time we would hear from and talk with some fifty-eight witnesses.

One of the first witnesses shared the results of a statewide emergency food program, conducted by local college faculty. The witness summarized their findings as depicting "an emerging catastrophe." More than two-thirds of the agencies reported hunger to be serious and growing as a problem in the state. Nearly 80 percent of administrators said responding to hunger is a major concern of their agency, sometimes the central concern.

What the agencies reported to us corresponded with this description. Ed Forster, a general in the Salvation Army, made the point well: "We have no leftovers. Requests for food are up by a third over the previous year, and twenty percent of the people have never before been to the Army for help." A representative of the St. Patrick's Church Pantry in Milford reported that their requests had doubled, and another from Operation Blessing in Portsmouth said theirs had increased by more than 100 percent. In Manchester, Greg Schneider's Food Pantry almost never got off the ground. "The first week our facility opened, 187 families applied for food. It immediately exhausted our supply."

Mark Manus of the Concord Chamber of Commerce reported that he was alarmed by the need. "Yes, the private sector can produce and distribute food among the hungry. But we realize this is not enough. We as a community no longer feel that we can ignore the problem of hunger." A representative of the state Public Health Department conveyed alarm about hunger in the state. Dietician Mindy Fitterman termed "very real" the hunger she and her colleagues saw in the homes of Peterborough, Manchester, Epsom, Hillsborough, and Concord. "No one made it up and it won't go away by itself. If you've not seen hunger in New Hampshire, just look around. I regularly see children whose hair is thin and dull instead of shiny and thick, and whose eyes have no sparkle." She said that many elderly who have chronic diseases and require special diets cannot get the food they need. "They are hurting, frustrated. Their golden years do not seem so golden."

Linda Hogan amplified on Mindy's remarks, referring to old people who try to get food from the WIC supplemental feeding program for mothers and babies. "I confronted an elderly woman who put formula in her purse. She told me that she was hungry."

Other elderly try to get by in other ways. Eighty-year-old Bradford Johnson of Gilsum told us that a typical day means eating cereal for breakfast, hamburger and potatoes for lunch, and soup for supper. "We go into the supermarket and look at what other people eat all the time and we can't afford it. The message we get is that we are not worthwhile."

As the testimony continued, others waiting to speak signed their names to the list at the door. While a nurse spoke to us, I noticed a commotion in the audience. Eyes turned toward the door where an elderly man on crutches made his way in through the crowd. Hardly waiting for the woman to finish, and totally disregarding the protocol for speakers, he made his way through the crowd of some three hundred people to stand before us. "Are you the doctors?" he demanded, as I signaled for someone to give him a chair.

"I heard on the radio you were coming here but I couldn't find the right room. I was afraid I'd miss you." He paused to catch his breath. "I'm sixty-five years old and my wife and I live up in the woods. Our ten-year-old car isn't so reliable, so I hitched rides to get here. I worked hard all my life. The Army turned me down 'cause of my bad leg, so I joined the National Guard during World War II. I worked in the shipyard 364 days a year, taking off only Christmas. Then I had to retire and we got into trouble. We don't have much to eat."

The old man's testimony took on the character of a private interview before a crowd of eavesdroppers. Undaunted, he told us how his wife was hungry and he felt he had to get her some food that day and he had no way to do so. Somehow we were the answer to his dilemma.

I quickly wrote a note to one of our staff, asking her to give the man twenty dollars for which I would reimburse her. I suggested that the man go outside to talk with people by the door who could assist him. He accepted my suggestion but not before a final comment to release his pent-up feelings.

"I'm a good American, but I'm angry enough today to understand why people become anarchists and communists. I feel like nobody when I walk into the welfare office. I'm treated like a liar and thief. I worked all my life, and I don't deserve this kind of treatment."

The old man placed the crutches under his arm, thanked us, and hobbled toward the door. The audience was hushed as I called for the next speaker.

Like the slow continuous beat of a drum, witness after witness appeared before us, hour after hour, nonstop throughout the morning and then the afternoon. At one point I almost called for a brief recess but decided against it after seeing how many people had signed up to speak to us. Periodically, I would catch myself trying to cut short my colleagues as they would ask questions of the people who spoke. But the steady flow of people before us created its own rhythm, and the process continued uninterrupted.

The Sisters of Mercy told about needy families who receive increased public assistance payments, only to find that their food stamps are decreased by the same amount. "In the end they're no better off," the Sister explained. "They can't get ahead."

Lloyd Littlefield of the state Education Department reported that 49 percent fewer school meals were served to children in the state due to federal cutbacks in the lunch program. "Yes, there is now hunger in New Hampshire," he concluded.

Valerie Long of the University of New Hampshire gave the results of their food consumption survey which revealed that a quarter of all state households were deficient in at least one critical vitamin. Significant numbers of older residents had nutritionally inadequate diets, and poor families seldom met minimal nutritional requirements. Ron Eskin of New Hampshire Legal Assistance followed Valerie to describe how food stamp regulations created in Washington make it virtually impossible for many needy families to get help, even though they qualify.

Sprinkled among these professionals were the parents, the children, and the old people who came to speak. Sometimes entire families would come up together, the children squirming and talking out loud as their parents answered our questions. Some parents would smile; others would cry. Usually they would thank us for listening and leave. Some asked where they could get food or a job.

One of the final witnesses of the day was Edward Wentzell, director of food services for the Plymouth School Department. He spoke for his own school system as well as others in the area, which he represented as part of a national school food service association. Ed described the growing numbers of hungry children in the schools and the efforts of school nurses to prevent anemia and malnutrition.

"In my opinion, Washington is leading this nation down a path when once again 'Hunger in America' will be the headline of tomorrow. It was a national disgrace when it happened before, and it will be no less so now."

Within a year ten national studies would confirm the man's prediction.

FROM NEW ENGLAND TO THE NATION

In early 1984 we held press conferences in Washington and Boston to issue a report of our findings in the region. Entitled *America Hunger Crisis: Poverty and Health in New England*, the document was of interest to the press because it was the first in-depth study of hunger in an entire region of the nation in at least two decades. I believe that their interest was also heightened because of the substantial number of prominent physicians participating in the undertaking and because we had opened our work to public scrutiny. By agreeing to let members of the press accompany us on our field visits, reporters were not in a position of merely accepting our analysis, but had seen the situation for themselves.

To our surprise, the report generated a great deal of national press attention. Its release was carried on the evening television network news, in major newspapers across the country, and in several hundred big-city and small-town papers.

In addition, members of Congress took notice of the study, registering concern about serious hunger in a region of the nation where the economy was relatively good. House Speaker Tip O'Neill had our study distributed to every member of the Congress, and several of us were invited to Washington to appear before committees of Congress to discuss our findings.

Our work aroused concern also among several national foundations, chief among them the Field and New World foundations. Under the direction of Dick Boone, the Field Foundation had been active for years in the areas of civil rights and advocacy for the poor. The Foundation had sponsored physician field studies in 1968 that had helped direct the nation's attention to the hunger and malnutrition that existed at the time. Several of my colleagues had participated in that work.

Dick Boone now feared the nation was slipping backwards, regressing to the situation that had existed before the government took an active role in nutrition programs for the poor. It was his idea that I expand my group of colleagues and study hunger in other regions of the nation. The Field Foundation awarded Harvard University a grant of $75,000 to support the work for one year. This money was matched by grants from other foundations. The funds were used primarily for travel, lodging, and staff salaries; all the doctors participated on a voluntary basis.

In the winter of 1984, I organized the Harvard Physician Task Force on Hunger in America, comprised primarily of nationally prominent doctors and public health experts. We emphasized participation from individuals with long-standing professional interest in hunger and malnutrition, as well as a diversity of political and regional views. We wanted to avoid any notion that partisan or geographic interests might motivate our conclusions. The Harvard School of Public Health was supportive as well, providing space for our offices and access to research materials.

Our scheduled work for the next year included field visits to eight states in the Deep South, the Mid-Atlantic region, the Southwest, and the Midwest. We would meet with political leaders, agency heads, health care providers, educators, emergency food providers, community organizations, and, of course, speak with hungry people themselves.

Although our goal was to gather facts and learn firsthand the experience of going hungry in a rich land, in the end we found we could not divorce our conclusions from the political setting in which we live. Our work would help to catalyze the largest community demonstration of public interest in our history, "Hands Across America," during which approximately six million people would form a human chain from New York to Los Angeles. And almost inevitably we would become the target of ideological forces that sought to discredit our work for political purposes.

2

A Killer in the Deep South

THE IMAGE of the baby remained vivid in my mind as I tried to sleep. She was the first thing I saw as I entered the dilapidated house in Greenwood, Mississippi, that morning, a tiny creature whose brown skin was dusty and uncovered. She lay whimpering on a torn mattress as her little brother tried to put an empty bottle in her mouth while swatting at the flies around her face.

An older girl stood in the doorway, silent and uncomfortable as the intruding doctors entered. Her father rose from his chair, gesturing to one of the visitors to take his seat, but no one moved. Behind him stood the mother, next to a pile of clothing that rose from the floor to the height of my eyes.

My mind raced to keep up with the visual images my eyes recorded: a small mass of humanity existing in a condemned house, with no front door, no windows, no plumbing, a worn sofa, two beds without covers, a dirty blanket piled on a chair, and a bright yellow balloon.

"These people are starving," said Joie Kammer, the seventy-seven-year-old worker from the St. Francis Center, our guide for the three-day field trip to the Mississippi Delta. The doctors had no reason to disagree. Joie had virtually adopted the family and had been supplying them with dried beans and other food items for several weeks. "It seems like I just can't do enough," Joie observed. "They got no job, no money, no food stamps."

In May 1984, government statistics placed unemployment in the area at 16 percent. A quarter of the state population lived in poverty, and very few of them received any aid. Some 300,000 poor residents were left out of the food stamp program. This family was among them.

They had subsisted on handouts for almost two months. Their food stamp application had been held up because the father could not verify his recent income. Employers did not pay him by check for his odd jobs, and federal rules designed to prevent cheating did not permit his personal declaration of income. "They're slowly starving," Joie repeated. "Sometimes I wish there could be a little bit of cheating so people like this could get food."

As we left I was the first to exit the house, more to relieve my senses than to keep the team of doctors on schedule. Stepping to avoid the hole in the porch, I turned to the parents as we left, but I found that I had no idea what to say. I muttered something and walked to the car.

"Just Like South Africa"

Everything is vivid in Mississippi. We drove down long roads of rich farmland, where cotton and soybean crops have been grown for two hundred years. Suddenly the panorama is broken by a stand of trees with a big house and several little shacks trailing off to the side, the homes for black families who have lived in the unheated dwellings for decades.

Signs proudly display the names of the plantations. Little attempt is made to hide, excuse, or change the enormous disparity between rich and poor in this state. Most of the residents have lived in this environment for so long that they defend it without shame. "There's no hunger here," one local physician told us, generalizing from his wealthy patients to the poor he never treats. "Every specimen I see is fat and shiny."

Hunger is easy to find for those willing to go into the homes of the poor. So are the other problems that accompany it, because people don't just get to be hungry in Mississippi without having other things wrong in their lives—dilapidated housing, no health care, no jobs. We saw substantial numbers of people whose lives are crippled by poverty and racism, lives that cannot be easily repaired. But the people we saw are also hungry, and that is a problem easier to remedy.

Our first field investigation outside the six New England states, Mississippi, had great historical significance. Perhaps the poorest state in the nation, it has for years symbolized poverty and degradation. So much so, in fact, that I hesitated to take our doctors there because Mississippi seemed more a stereotype than a reality. It is easy to dismiss the state as an uncharacteristic quirk of American history and racial bigotry. But Mississippi, like other Southern states, had experienced noticeable progress in the 1970s, including fewer hungry people. Some of my colleagues on this trip had been responsible for that.

I had flown into the state with Bill Beardslee and Gordon Harper, friends and physicians in the Harvard medical community who had been to Mississippi in the sixties and seventies to look into hunger and malnutrition. Beardslee, the son of a well-to-do Atlanta family, had registered voters in the South during his college days. Subsequently he and Gordon Harper returned to the state with a team of doctors sent out by the Field Foundation to provide a firsthand report on hunger in the region. Gordon, a Harvard-educated child psychiatrist now working as a clinician at Children's Hospital psychiatric clinic, was among those who had seen a substantial change in the hunger problem in Mississippi as the result of federal assistance in the last two decades.

Our team included two more senior members, both Mississippi natives. Aaron Shirley, chairman of the Mississippi Medical and Surgical Association, has lived in the state his entire life. As a black physician practicing in a clinic in Jackson, Aaron has been part of recent history. On three occasions, first in 1968, he has been a member of physician teams sent across the nation to assess the problem of hunger. Quiet, unassuming, a man with an abiding belief in justice, he has channeled his legitimate anger into constructive purpose.

Aaron had been among the first physicians I called when I assembled a panel of prominent doctors to address America's most recent hunger problem. "Why another study?" he asked me, questioning whether national leaders were really open to factual documentation. Aaron had been one of the doctors who minced no words in their report to Congress in 1968. "We do not want to quibble over words, but 'malnutrition' is not quite what we found. . . . They are suffering from hunger and disease and directly or indirectly they are dying from them—which is exactly what 'starvation' means."

Ken Dean, a white Baptist minister who had organized the 1968 Field investigation, was one of two non-physicians in our group. Ken is an imposing figure, physically as well as morally. Unorthodox and irascible, he envisions the role of a minister as a broad one. He takes the Biblical message of administering unto the poor and needy quite literally.

With colorful words and Southern phrases coming from behind the cigar in his mouth, Ken had led a team of United States senators and doctors to the Delta in 1968. In a state of shock, conservative Republican Senator George Murphy at the time had muttered: "I didn't know that we were going to be dealing with the situation of starving people and starving youngsters."

What the senators saw, and what the doctors reported, later moved a nation. During the course of several years two Presidents and Congress responded to the problem of hunger. The food stamp program was expanded so poor families could purchase food. School lunch and breakfast programs were increased so children could have adequate nutrition while they learned. Feeding programs for the elderly were developed to reach isolated older Americans in homes and rural communities. And the supplemental feeding program for women, infants and children (WIC) was established to increase birth weights and decrease the death rate among babies in America.

The colleagues who accompanied me on this return trip had been part of that history, a story of success. Ten years later, in 1977, they had returned to the Mississippi Delta and several other states to see the results of their labor. Where they had once seen malnourished children and listless elderly people living on the brink of starvation, the doctors saw nutrition programs that were working. Poor people were still poor; they still lived in decrepit housing. But they had food in their pantries. Teachers said that the school meals made a big difference for their students. Doctors found much less malnutrition. To be certain, things were not perfect but they were greatly improved. As the junior member of the team, I was now in the disconcerting position of leading a group of veterans back to an area they knew so well to find out why hunger had reappeared.

Once word leaked out that a group of "Harvard doctors" was going to Mississippi to investigate the return of hunger, we began to receive inquiries from the press. Among the first to sign on for the trip were Steve Curwood of the *Boston Globe* and two national network news correspondents from NBC and CBS. Enlarging the pool more were reporters from

Jackson and local communities we were to visit. Altogether we looked like a presidential entourage of some sort, a factor we would encounter again and again as we traveled across the nation. Sometimes the large delegation made our work cumbersome; often we split our group of doctors into teams, partly for work efficiency and partly to disperse the number of press covering our trip. But overall we were committed to conducting our work under the watchful eyes of the press, knowing that it was important for them to see for themselves the hunger we were finding.

People start lining up outside the food stamp office in Greenwood at eight o'clock each morning, a half hour before the doors open. Those waiting appeared pretty evenly divided between children, parents, and elderly people. The press, accompanied by several Mississippi physicians, had arrived before our team. People stared at the unusual bustle and commotion our entrance caused.

As the early spring sun began to bear down I noticed the sweat beading on the faces of the doctors and their unwitting patients. We worked the line separately or in twos, mingling with the local people to learn of their circumstances. It was the last day of the month and food stamps had been exhausted for recipients for several days. Some had eaten with friends recently. More had cut down to one meal a day, usually chicken neckbones or beans. Others had not eaten for several days, and came early to be first in line to get their stamps.

We concentrated on babies being held by mothers, who told us some of the infants had had no milk for three, four, even five days. Aaron had warned us we would find severe deprivation; Mississippi children are frequently deficient in vital nutrients like vitamins A and C, iron and protein. Thinking about this, I overheard two elderly women acknowledging that they had had nothing to eat for "maybe three or four days, it's kinda hard to remember."

People waiting for coupons in order to eat hardly seemed like America. It wasn't like anything I had seen before in my

New England travels. David Levy, a physician from the University of Mississippi Medical School and a white South African, was visibly shaken by what he witnessed, later saying it reminded him of scenes of hunger in his native land.

As the line of hungry people pressed against the brightly colored wall of the one-story food stamp office, Naomi Kistin, a pediatrician from Chicago, edged closer to comment that she was glad *NBC Nightly News* was recording the event: "At least I will be less likely to dismiss this as a bad dream." I nodded without responding.

We made our way inside as the door opened, following the people who rushed to take seats in the reception room, only to wait another hour or two to be seen. Several colleagues continued to talk with the people who came for help while three of us went in to see Chris Murphree, the local food stamp director. Ms. Murphree remembered having been interviewed by several of my companions on their Delta trip almost a decade earlier. She was in the same job; I speculated to myself that she was even behind the same desk as she had been then. But other things had changed.

The day before, Murphree's boss, the director of Hines County Welfare Department, had told us that the need for emergency food assistance had nearly doubled during the past year. "People just can't survive off the food stamp amount," she reported, "it's just not adequate." When we mentioned her boss's admission, Murphree relaxed, realizing she was free to give us her unvarnished view of the problem she sees every day.

"Food stamps don't last," she conceded, attributing hunger in the area to that fact as well as to what she termed "complications." She described the paperwork—endless forms to fill out and entries to verify—that eliminated some people from the process even while their families went without food. "The government requires a lot of extra paperwork now," she continued, "and in my view it's for nothing. It doesn't do anything but keep people from getting help."

As if to express a feeling within us all that things in the past were simpler, she said that when she began her job years ago there were just three pages to fill out in order to apply for food stamps. She handed us an application packet which was six pages long, accompanied by nine other forms along with yet another form, which looked like an income tax statement, to be completed monthly by the recipients.

"How can people handle all these requirements?" Gordon asked. Some of those in line were young, others very old, and many only semiliterate, a fact we had learned when some asked us to interpret forms they held in their hands while waiting in line. Murphree conceded the point, adding that not only do these forms represent a formidable hurdle, but that many recipients have to return to her office during the month to bring yet other forms or to pick up food stamps. Those who have jobs have to take time off to come in; others simply can't make it in and find themselves cut off the program.

Ken Dean whispered to me as we left the office: "Did you see that damn pile of forms? Now you tell me how those people sitting there with empty bellies are going to get food today!" I looked at him without saying anything. We knew most of them probably wouldn't eat

Aaron's impression was more complex than ours, being rooted in fifty years of personal experience living in Mississippi, over half of them providing medical care to the poor. He saw a similarity between the food stamp program and the old plantation system. On the typical plantation there is the white owner, the white overseer and the black tenant farmer, Aaron explained. The tenant farmer and family are at the mercy of the overseer, who reports directly to the owner. The owner's interest is best served by a docile tenant, and in order to maintain this state of mind it is better to discourage education and knowledge. The owner controls the local public schools that the tenant farmer's children attend, if they attend at all, and the owner's children attend a private, segregated academy.

The overseer is frequently the tenant farmer's major contact with creditors, places of business, legal assistance, and much of the world outside the plantation. He influences everything from voting to seeking justice and petitioning for better schools and educational opportunities.

Now comes the food stamp program with its complex organizational structure and administration. The white county welfare director takes on the role of being the plantation owner, the welfare case worker the role of the overseer, and the black food stamp recipient continues in the role of tenant farmer. The same conditions and forces prevail, with the attending adverse effects, that existed on the old plantation.

"THE FACES OF DEATH"

We were taken by the volunteer drivers to McClure's Alley, which is not really an alley, but a short dead-end dirt road within the town of Greenwood. Rows of six or seven houses face one another on each side. With white shacks with peeling paint and children sitting on the porches next to old-fashioned wringer washing machines, the place looked like something out of a Faulkner novel.

Standing in the center of the dusty road, Joie called out to the residents who knew her as the social worker at the St. Francis Center: "We got here a group of doctors who have come from up North to talk to you about your problems," she drawled. "They're good people, so let them in to talk with you and tell them what they want to know."

We split into small groups, some going inside the houses and others talking with people on their porches. Gordon and I briefly spoke to a youngster playing in front of his home before a camera crew filming our conversation scared him into silence.

We approached a woman on her porch; she was perhaps seven months pregnant. Her other child listened as we explained who we were. The mother had lost a baby the year before but didn't know exactly what caused the death. Her total monthly income consisted of $60 in food stamps, on which she tried to feed herself, her unborn child and a five-year-old son. We asked to go in the house, thinking she might be embarrassed to talk in front of the ever-present cameras. However, the camera crew followed us in as we went to the kitchen.

After asking permission, Gordon opened the refrigerator to find three sticks of butter. In a cupboard were some dried beans. Nothing more to eat was in the house. The woman had had no milk for several days and her son had a cup the day before. She answered questions but ventured no information otherwise.

"When did you last have milk?" I asked.

"Day or two ago," she answered.

"How about your son?"

"Yesterday morning. He had a little yesterday morning."

"Are you hungry?" I asked.

"Yes, sir."

"Do you have any food besides the dried beans?"

"No, sir."

Formal politeness, no anger, no effort to tell it all. Nothing about her fears, about the infant she carried. Nothing about the baby who had died a year before.

"What you're looking at are the faces of infant mortality statistics," I remarked to Steve Curwood, who asked me what I thought about what we had seen. The faces behind the numbers that appear in government mortality data were staring at us from the porches of this little street. Steve nodded; one did not have to be a medical expert to see the connection.

After an hour of talking with residents of the Alley, we were urged to leave in order to keep up with the itinerary Joie had planned for the day. But several members of the team mutinied, heading for houses on nearby streets to knock on doors unannounced. Led by Ken Dean, who spent years knocking on doors talking to people in the state, I later learned that a few of the doctors felt angry. They thought Joie had "set us up," that she had picked the worst place in town to take us and that it did not fairly represent the picture of need.

I sent one car on ahead to our next destination and remained with the maverick team. Later we joined our colleagues, having been convinced by the empty pantries we had seen in some seven or eight houses that people were indeed out of food. Later one of the doctors confided that he had been so upset by what he saw that he took his anger out on Joie rather than the unseen hands that allow such tragedy to exist in our nation. I never mentioned this to Joie but somehow I thought she would understand if she knew.

An hour later the change of location brought different skin color but not radically different circumstances. We met seventy-year-old Emma Ferris, who lived in an apartment and, by her own description, used to be middle-class. Photographs around her apartment seemed to confirm her life had once been more comfortable.

Bill Beardslee spoke with her at length, learning that Emma had been cut off the supplemental security income program for reasons she did not quite understand. When her daughter died of leukemia she sold her car, and this "income" apparently made her ineligible. She was to repay the money but had no income to do so. As she described her situation her grandmotherly disposition masked the problems she faced. While Bill spoke to her I opened the refrigerator to find four eggs, bread, mayonnaise, and a jar of honey.

Emma Ferris cannot walk, but she is a resourceful woman. She somehow managed to plant a small garden that she was hoping would provide more food than she had on the day we visited her in May. How, we asked, does she get outside to the garden? We were startled to hear her answer: "I crawl."

I remember feeling as if I could crawl from the house of this woman. So stressed did I feel at what we were finding in the Delta that I felt overwhelmed, but Ms. Ferris somehow made me ashamed to succumb to it all. She faced difficulty every day; she had little food, she couldn't even walk, yet she maintained a pleasant disposition even if her tone masked what the psychiatrist with me found to be deep depression.

Throughout the afternoon teams of doctors fanned out across the tiny towns which dot the Delta: Money, Tutweiler, Marks, and Ita Bena. Some were obscure places, sleepy villages whose rich histories were hiding the pain and suffering of several generations. Some had briefly captured national attention during the civil rights struggles of the 1960s, only to fade again into obscurity. "See that gas station over there?" one of the local guides said as he pointed across the street from a Headstart center we visited. "Gasoline station" was too kind a description for the two old-fashioned pumps under the overhanging roof that covered an asphalt area dotted by weeds that had burst free of the coating. I couldn't tell whether the station operated anymore, but its memory still lingered as the guide explained its historical importance. Nearly three decades before, a fifteen-year-old black boy named Emett Till allegedly whistled at a white woman who had come for gasoline. Shortly afterwards he was found dead, his bullet-riddled body in a nearby river. The Ku Klux Klan had taken retaliatory action against the youngster to protect the honor of white women in the area, and the execution had made national headlines.

The group of doctors was moved by recalling this bit of sad historical drama, but most realized that untimely death for other residents may be less dramatic, but just as certain. Maxine Hays, a petite black pediatrician born in the state and now a colleague of mine at Harvard, found the conditions shocking. "I thought I was familiar with the poverty and hunger here," she admitted, "but the degree of it is just overwhelming."

Maxine and Naomi made a house call to the Yates family, a white couple with three children living on a plantation near Phillips. Jerry, the father, brings home just over two dollars an hour working as a farmhand. The family gets some food stamps but has no medical coverage. Two of the children have seizure disorders that require regular medications which the family cannot afford. They owe $5,000 at the county hospital for one stay the prior autumn.

"After we pay for rent, utilities, and medical bills there ain't much left," the mother noted. "The kids get hungry, but what can I do?"

Maxine inquired about the metal barrel which served as a wood stove. It looked like an accident waiting to happen, being neither safe nor efficient. "We all sleep in one room during the winter," the mother offered. "Last year we lost our house to a fire."

Nearby lived seventy-six-year-old Laura Jane Allen, who had a social security income of $189 and got a bonus of $10 in food stamps. For days before our arrival she had eaten only peas, beans, and bread. Her weight was down considerably.

"How are you feeling?" Naomi inquired.

"Well, I got high blood pressure, I guess. The doctor, he say I'm suppose' to have fresh vegetables and fish, and to stay away from salt." The old woman paused before completing her response. "But I jus' can't buy them things on my money."

Laura Jane continued to eat what she could afford, a diet rich in the things which bring an earlier death. She was already older than most, but her health was going downhill for no good reason. We had seen many others that day who were far younger, who were experiencing the same fateful process. Hunger had become a real killer in the Delta.

"WE'RE DEALING WITH PEOPLE'S SURVIVAL"

We assembled that night in a storage building for a public hearing. Through flyers and by word of mouth, residents of the area had heard that doctors from the North were coming and that they wanted to talk to people about their problems. The large hall was crowded with 250 to 300 people, mostly black residents of the area. Some children were present, out-

numbered by the large number of elderly. Some entire families attended, as well as local professionals who try to respond
to the needs of the people they see.

I introduced myself and my colleagues, although Aaron
Shirley seemed well-known to many who nodded as I mentioned his name. Though he lives ninety miles away, his name
in the Delta is linked to any number of efforts to alleviate
suffering among its poorer residents. I told the audience that
we were there to hear from them, that we did not believe
hunger has a place in America and we wanted to learn of their
situation. My few words of introduction turned into several
minutes and could have developed into a sermon judging from
the chorus of "amens" that punctuated my statements. I suddenly felt like the minister's son that I had been while growing
up, rather than the Harvard professor I had become. Quickly
I set up a procedure for people to testify and started the
evening.

A white woman who identified herself as a local pediatrician marched to the chair in front of our table. "I am Dr.
Marilyn Barker," she began, "and last week I watched a baby
die of malnutrition."

Dr. Barker reported that during the past several years
more patients were coming for emergency care, a lot of them
because they had been cut from the Medicaid or AFDC (Aid
to Families with Dependent Children) programs due to changes
in federal policies. Her colleague, the health officer for eight
counties in the Delta, corroborated the seriousness of health
and living conditions among the people there: "What we need
are jobs and no more budget cuts," Dr. Rousa began. "The
problems of the Delta are social problems," he explained,
"not just health problems."

I could not help but notice the impassioned manner in
which one local professional addressed us, almost pleading for
someone to listen. Psychiatrist Kenlock Gil spoke as if to spill
out the agony he sees daily in his mental health center. "We're
dealing with people's survival," Dr. Gil announced. "When

you talk about poverty around here you're talking about poverty! Part of our mental health service is to help people get food stamps."

Nearly half the caseload at the mental health center was unemployed at the time, and 72 percent had family income under $149 weekly. Gil reported that his staff sees a high rate of retardation due to hunger and malnutrition. "We can't really do our job well due to the risk factors of malnutrition, poverty, and bad housing. Things were getting better in the sixties and seventies, but now they're getting worse again."

How bad things are in the Delta seemed well-known to Joyce Stanson, a registered nurse who spoke for the patients she visits in their homes. With a calm passion she sat before us without notes: "My elderly patients are hungry. They're starving at home. Many of them have chronic diseases and they never come out. They sit there and slowly starve." The chorus of "amens" echoed again. A mass of poor people listened as the young nurse gave an unadulterated account of what she sees every day in her work, and they knew she was speaking for them. "Amen," they continued.

Stanson's impassioned statement seemed to give others courage to speak up. A middle-aged woman approached the table. "I'm Mrs. Johnson, and I just wanted to say that I'm hungry. Thank you," she added as she walked back to her seat. No crying, no analysis, no one to blame. "You doctors want to know how we are," she seemed to be saying. "We're hungry."

Not everyone who suffered did it so quietly. Others told of being cut off the food stamp program due to federal changes in rules. Some felt harassed by local bureaucracy. Still others spoke of the difficulty of getting jobs in a region where unemployment is so high.

Mr. Campbell strode to the podium. "I'm not hungry, but I know plenty of people who are. I know them by name: Laura, Mary, Hattie . . . they live right near me. It's sort of like the old days again." The old man's last comment was bewildering, but he went on to explain it as he addressed his own needs: "There's a limit to the number of times I can see my doctor," he said. "Unusual things happen to your body when you get old and this morning I needed to go back to see him. I remembered the days when we used to have to get permission from the boss man before the doctor would see us. So's I got scared and didn't go." I recalled Aaron's description of the plantation mentality and how it still affects so many aspects of life in the Deep South.

Upon our arrival in Mississippi, the Governor had frankly admitted that hunger and poverty were serious problems in the state. He said that initially he had been pleased the previous fall when President Reagan's Task Force on Food Assistance had scheduled a visit to his state following our report to Congress. The Governor had instructed his staff to cooperate with the Presidential commission and had assembled files of data and expert testimony from health providers for their review. But when the Reagan Task Force arrived its members seemed more interested in the Southern-style grits-and-eggs breakfast that had been prepared for them at the Governor's mansion. After eating, the President's team left the state, never once making a home visit or talking to a medical professional. The Governor told us he had been deeply dismayed and angered by the Presidential Task Force, feeling that "the lives of so many of our people were lost or forgotten on the way back to the White House."

I did not want to make the same mistake, so when I returned to Boston I wrote to the two congressmen chiefly responsible for federal hunger programs in the House, Representatives Leon Panetta of California and Mickey Leland of Texas. I told them that we had discovered a desperate situation in Mississippi and urged them and their colleagues to go to the Delta immediately to see the situation for themselves.

The congressmen were responsive to my letter, although the circumstances of their going gave me a glimpse into the politics that permits hunger to exist in this country. Representatives Panetta and Leland had seen national press coverage of our trip to Mississippi and, I felt, understood that a very serious situation exists there. But several of their colleagues were not as easy to convince, especially after they learned that Panetta had asked me to accompany the Congressional team back to the area.

Press reports of our initial trip disturbed several Republican members of the House Select Committee on Hunger. One of their colleagues, Representative Webb Franklin, was in a reelection contest in the Delta. In an effort not to undercut Congressman Franklin, a white Republican who was being challenged by a black Democrat, several members of the Committee said they would not go to Mississippi "unless the Harvard doctors stay at home."

While I was amused to learn that these politicians found our presence so threatening, I was angry that seasoned members of Congress would place politics above life-threatening conditions in the Delta. At first I refused to back out of the trip; I wanted to be certain that the members—Republicans as well as Democrats—saw what we had seen and came face to face with the hungry people we had discovered. But I also knew that for their investigation to be credible the Congressional committee had to have a mixture of Republicans and Democrats. If the Democrats went alone, the Republicans were likely to dismiss the field trip as political in order to protect the reelection chances of their colleague.

Finally I learned that Representatives Bill Emerson of Missouri and Marge Roukema of New Jersey, the only Republicans scheduled to go on the trip, refused to go unless I backed out. Panetta and Leland left the decision to me, assuring me that the trip would be a serious endeavor whether I went or not. I wanted the Republicans to see what the Democrats would see, so I backed out. But that was not the last hitch in the plans.

In a unique form of courtesy that borders on the feudal,

Congressional committees generally do not go into the district of another member unless that member first gives permission. Representative Franklin, a two-term congressman from the Delta, had not given permission for this trip and from all reports was not inclined to do so. Apparently, he was angry that our earlier trip had generated so much publicity about hunger and malnutrition among his constituents. Moreover, his opponent had charged him with supporting the federal budget cuts that had made the situation in the Delta even worse. In short, our effort to get members of Congress to look into a desperate situation in Mississippi was being stymied due to electoral politics.

I was furious. It was one thing for me to drop out of the Congressional visit in order to enable it to go forth; it was another to have the trip canceled because an embarrassed politician was unwilling to see the effect of the policies he had supported. I picked up the phone and called the editor of the local paper in Greenwood, Mississippi, suggesting that he look into this situation. Soon afterwards the paper carried a story on the controversy.

Franklin then wrote a letter, back-dated two weeks, to the House Select Committee on Hunger requesting that the Committee come into his district to conduct an investigation. He wanted it to appear as if the idea had been his in the first place. When his House colleagues arrived, Franklin gave an impassioned speech about his concern over hunger in the Mississippi Delta. He was subsequently reelected by a small margin, and I have often wondered how many politicians, like him, engage in the most dishonest endeavors while appearing to be concerned about justice for people they are elected to represent.

On the first day of their Mississippi field visit, I was later to learn, Congressman Panetta walked over to two young girls standing in McClure's Alley watching the House members and the press. He said hello to the children and received a greeting in unison. "Are you happy that school is out?" he

asked, anticipating the affirmative response one would expect
at the start of summer vacation. When one of the girls said
no, they were not glad about school ending, Panetta pursued
the matter by asking why not. "Because," the child answered,
"when we is in school we gets to eat lunch, but in summer
we only gets supper."

These girls represent the face of hunger in Mississippi.
They are not starving, at least not in the sense that we see
starvation in foreign lands. But they are hungry, and they are
easy to find.

ALABAMA: "WRETCHED BEYOND ACCEPTABILITY"

George Corley Wallace shifted in his wheelchair and pulled
himself closer to his governor's desk in the Montgomery state
capitol. "Yankee doctors," he said with a slight smile on his
face as he glanced at the physicians around his desk. "You
know, I been up North before, but why you coming down
here to see us?"

We had left Mississippi only the day before, and I sus-
pected that the Alabama Governor knew more about our visit
than he acknowledged. A man who had sworn that the schools
in his state would never be integrated, and who had taken a
stab at defying the federal government to back up his pledge,
Wallace had come to national prominence years ago, when
I was in college. But time had caught up with Governor Wallace. Standing behind him, two feet from me, was his chief
aide, a young black man who smiled at the Governor's toying
with us.

As his banter turned more serious I recalled the many
times this national figure had lashed out against "pointy-headed
intellectuals." The Governor fiddled nervously with his pencil, pushed his wheelchair back and forth, and seemed to size
us up. His monologue was effusive, stressing the self-suffi-
ciency of the state, the incompetence of the federal govern-

ment as he saw it, the way Northerners always castigate the South, and how he loves blacks and whites equally.

I tried to put the Governor at ease by telling him first of the extent of hunger and malnutrition we had found in New England states. I found myself acknowledging that I had been born in Decatur, a northern Alabama city, even though I had lived there for only the first six months of my life. The tactic worked. Suddenly, while I was not a real "down-home boy," the Governor understood that I was not a Harvard professor coming to make fun of Southern ways. He began to tell us of the problems among his constituents.

Hungry people are all over Alabama, Wallace told us, "especially since the federal government cut the food stamp program." He asked what we might do to help expose the problem and then offered to assist us in our efforts. Before leaving the capitol, I had been made Honorary Lieutenant Colonel in the Alabama Militia and was offered direct access to the Governor himself as needed.

Alabama is a more industrialized state than Mississippi, with the major urban centers of Montgomery, Birmingham, and Huntsville running south to north. But outside the steel and industrial plants lie some of the most impoverished counties of the nation—Lowndes and Butler to the south, and Choctow, Green, Pickins, and Sumpter on the Mississippi border to the west.

We selected the state because of its diverse economy and extremes of wealth and poverty. The state was also of a personal interest to me, since it had been home to my close friend John Lewis, long-time civil rights activist and now a congressman from Atlanta. The son of a tenant farmer, John taught himself public speaking by preaching to the chickens in his father's henhouse. He is a quiet and unassuming man who has been arrested more than forty times leading sit-ins at lunch counters and other public facilities. On the Selma March in 1964, John nearly lost his life when his skull was fractured by a policeman's club.

John Lewis had described to me the hunger he had seen as a child and the abject poverty many people face in rural Alabama. Conditions had improved during his lifetime, but there were now reports that growing numbers of people in the state were hungry. We wanted to see for ourselves.

I divided our doctors into teams to cover different regions of the state; we were to reconvene several days later in Birmingham. Some went by car into the rural western counties, where they met with local doctors, health center staff, ministers, and teachers. As we had done in Mississippi, they went into scores of homes to talk with families, to look into pantries, and to hear how people lived. Other task force members went to southern counties and to adjoining Montgomery.

Several outstanding Alabama physicians joined us in our work, but Dr. George Pickett was central to our understanding the region. Associate Dean of the University of Alabama School of Public Health, George had used his clinical skills as a pediatrician in a number of settings. But his chief contribution was in the area of public policy.

"Wretched beyond acceptability," he termed the general environment in which poor babies and their families live in Alabama. The infant mortality rate for the state had actually gone up the previous year and was at morally unacceptable levels in several individual counties. The rate of 31 infant deaths per thousand births in Hale County, for example, is almost three times the national rate and worse than rates for a number of developing nations. Ten percent of Alabama babies have low birth weight, a dangerous condition associated with poor nutrition for the mother.

The day we arrived was particularly wretched as a series of tornadoes ripped through the area, killing several people and bringing torrential rains and darkness. As radio announcers told of danger and encouraged people to stay in their homes, we made our way to a Salvation Army soup kitchen where more than one hundred men, women, and children had braved the storm in order to get a meal. Captain Price told us that he had taken sandwiches to outlying counties hit earlier by the tornadoes and found, to his astonishment, that many of the people had not eaten the previous day, either. This was not because of the storm; their refrigerators were empty.

As the press listened to the Captain talk to my colleagues, I spotted a young man whose stomach seemed empty. He had gobbled his meal and eyed the remaining pots of food at the serving table. No, there was not enough for seconds, he was told, as the timid courage he mustered proved unavailing. The father of three children and a baby, this unemployed steelworker and his wife had agreed five months earlier that he should leave Birmingham to look for work elsewhere. Alabama is one of many states that provides no public assistance to unemployed families if the father is in the home. I pondered the utter stupidity of federal policy, which makes families break apart in order to get help. I wondered what it was doing to this family.

"I have children, too," I said. "I imagine you miss yours, having to be so far away."

"I misses them, mister . . ." he said. "I misses them a lot." The tears in his eyes made me wish I had never asked. To cover my uneasiness, I tried to talk more, saying that I supposed any father would miss his children. Staring into the empty plate, the man nodded: "I cried too many times to have more tears."

This man never talks to his children; they have no phone. But he told me he writes them, "So they'll know I'm thinking about them." He sleeps wherever he can, the riverbank having been his bed the previous night. He thought he had a job the next day cutting grass for a lady, but he wouldn't know for sure until the evening. Eyeing the press who were several feet away, I reached into my pocket in as inconspicuous a manner as possible. When I thought it was okay, I handed the man a bill and told him I would remember him. I was sure, I said, that things would get better. I did not feel like I was telling the truth.

The Salvation Army in Montgomery serves a lot of families, elderly and middle-aged people; the soup kitchen guests look like a cross section of America in that sense. According to the Captain in charge, this is the only meal of the day for a quarter of the people, and demand for help increases monthly. "The economy has picked up for business," he observed, "but it hasn't helped the poor."

Rosa Smith is poor. This eighty-three-year-old woman is blind in one eye and lives on social security and disability payments, a total income of $334 monthly. As we sat in her living room, with its linoleum-covered floor, I asked her why she no longer got food stamps. "I don't know, they never told me. They just cut me off." I wondered if anyone in Washington could possibly justify denying food stamps to a blind old woman living on social security.

Leaving Rosa's, we went by car to the home of Phoebe Ellington, ten years younger and a resident of a housing project in Gainesville. Phoebe does get food stamps—$52 a month to supplement her husband's pension of $177. Her empty refrigerator starkly revealed the drama that takes place in their home toward the end of each month. For three days she had lived on corn bread and ketchup.

Phoebe came to mind again when Doris Ingram of the Montgomery Council on Aging later told us that hunger is a "sleeping giant" that awaits elderly people in the region. A spouse's death, unexpected medical costs—anything out of the ordinary—and the elderly become destitute. Their meager budgets don't stretch. Food becomes the expendable item. "These are the formerly productive Americans," Ingram pointed out, "who helped build these great United States.'"

"CORN FLAKES AND WATER"

Patricia Jones was not yet elderly, but she, too, knew the pain of hunger. Having recently moved from Georgia with her three-year-old son, this mother opened her refrigerator at my request: three eggs, a slice of cheese, a container of water. I asked if her son ate the corn flakes sitting in the box atop the refrigerator. "Yes sir, sometimes," she answered, "but he don't much like them with water." How long, I inquired, since he had milk to drink? "Three weeks," she answered, "since before we moved."

Mrs. Jones told us she had been receiving food stamps in Georgia before coming to Montgomery. When she moved to Alabama she had filled out several forms and made several inquiries about the fact she had been unable to receive assistance, but her efforts had produced no positive results. Since her arrival she and her son had been dependent for food on Catholic Social Services and the help of some neighbors. When she had called the food stamp office to let them know a team of doctors and reporters would be visiting her home, she was supplied with an emergency allotment of food stamps. We were pleased our presence could provide a bright spot in an otherwise dark and rainy day.

The next day Gordon Harper and I left with our volunteer driver to go to the Jones Day Care Center in a residential Montgomery neighborhood. Run by a matronly woman in her home, the center was two pleasant-looking rooms filled with young children at small tables. The youngsters ranged in age from two to four years. On his lap, Gordon held one child, a girl just over three years old according to the director. She had the body of a child eighteen months old. She sat listlessly, looking at the floor as Gordon tried to capture her attention. Each time he removed his hand from her back she started to lose her balance.

"She eats a lot on Monday mornings," reported the woman.

"That morning meal is all some of them gets." Most of the children were not as lethargic as this child, but many of them are hungry when they aren't in her program. "It's that way all around here," she assured us. "Go and see for yourselves."

Leaving our guide, we followed her suggestion and walked across the street to knock on doors at random. It was a style of investigating we had learned in McClure's Alley, and one we would later employ in our travels across the nation. A mother of two children, ages four and one year, confided that she was unemployed. She got no food stamps. She had milk in the refrigerator, but no food. "How are you folks getting by?" Gordon asked. "We're doing okay, really, just got no food." As we pressed we learned that a health center doctor had recently told her both children are anemic.

"Doing okay"—with empty refrigerators. That would be a theme we would hear again and again as we went into homes there and in other states. I don't recall a "complainer," anyone who seemed to be waiting to tell us how badly off he was. But if we were patient, when we took the time to probe, we found the suffering, the pain, sometimes the anger.

Betty Childs summarized the feelings of several mothers we talked with in the living room of a housing project. She described their struggle, some almost making a full-time job of hunting for sales, shopping with children in tow, without a car, walking to soup kitchens and back home. She admitted frequent failure . . . and anger: "A lot of people here are hungry. When you see people on TV saying there are no problems in this land of plenty, you get angry because they are lying."

Mrs. Miles, the Head Start bus driver in Lee County, understood the anger. She said she sees a lot of hungry children every morning. Some cry. Some are nauseated. Others act up. Dorothy Bunbridge, who runs St. Jude's Social Services, sees it too, growing numbers of families with children, but without food. "Some families have eaten nothing for twenty-four hours," she assured us, "and that includes the children."

A lot of them, according to agency records, have been cut from the food stamp program for technical reasons.

"The Game Is to Beat up on the Poor"

We were reaching the unmistakable conclusion that recent federal budget cuts in nutrition programs were devastating for poor Alabamans. Naomi Kistin reminded us of the official rhetoric that promised that corporations would pick up where government had pulled out. Clearly, this was not materializing. As she put it, "We don't seem to be finding private industry doing much of anything to respond to these problems."

Because of her position as the Director of the Alabama Family Health Administration, Beverly Boyd could be even more specific. "Everything that helps people in Alabama is federal dollars. The state was hit with federal budget cuts at a time when there was high unemployment and an economic downturn. We just couldn't make it up."

At the state food stamp office in Montgomery, supervisor Sarah Lund told us that poverty in the state had increased dramatically, but the number of families assisted by her program had actually decreased. A middle-aged woman who has worked for years in public service, Lund emphasized that the "tone set in Washington" had made life more difficult for the hungry families, a view remarkably like that of Chris Murphree at the food stamp office in Greenwood, Mississippi. Lund added that new regulations from Washington had forced them to terminate their outreach programs in order to divert staff to a "fraud unit" assigned to look for cheaters. Lund said there are few cheaters, but federal officials make political hay on the issue: "The game in Washington is to beat up on the poor."

Larry Gardella, a young staff attorney at Alabama Legal Services, went on to cite examples of this new attitude. He pointed out that, "No one told our elderly clients they could deduct the cost of their medicines from their income when they applied for food stamps. This means that many of them, even though they are needy and hungry, show an income over the eligibility standard for the food stamp program.

"Federal rules require evidence that one is job searching," he went on, laughing as he spoke. "Just about everyone around here—young or old—would give their right arm for a job. Those same federal rules require people to go off nine or ten miles for a bogus job interview, so they look good on the federal forms." Many of his clients did not have a car or transportation money. Yet if they failed to go on such interviews they would not get food stamps.

"THROUGH THE SAFETY NET"

On our last day in Alabama, we attended a public hearing at the state Capitol. Before hearing from the people who came to tell their stories, we listened to a number of state officials. I dreaded this task, thinking it would be boring; I wanted to go right to the audience, but found that my impatience was not justified. The officials showed a remarkable understanding of the hunger faced by citizens in the state.

Dr. Leon Frazier, the Commissioner of the Department of Pensions and Security, painted a graphic portrait of widespread insecurity in Alabama. Describing the food stamp program as the "bulwark against hunger," this scholarly looking black official of about fifty years of age explained how federal policy changes meant that fewer people got stamps even though poverty was increasing. Without notes he recited the numbers of Alabama residents hurt by new laws and regulations in Washington: programs delivering meals to the homebound elderly had been terminated; thousands of children from low-income families had been cut from the school lunch program; and elimination of federal block grants had required the state to eliminate still other services that federal money had once provided. "Hunger and malnutrition are definitely with us,"

Frazier reported. "There's just not enough to help these people. The safety net has fallen through."

I interrupted Dr. Frazier's testimony to ask about the father I had met in the Salvation Army Soup Kitchen. How, I queried, could a man who supported his family all his life become unemployed due to layoffs and then be denied public assistance to feed his kids until he got back on his feet? I asked him if he could help me see the logic of requiring a father to leave home in order for the family to qualify for AFDC (Aid to Families with Dependent Children).

Frazier did not dispute the meanness in the situation to which I referred. He explained that the federal government does not require all states to aid families if the unemployed father is in the home. Consequently, some states have chosen to "save money" by making intact families ineligible for this assistance. Alabama is one of them. Twenty-five other states do the same. Frazier acknowledged that while this may be popular politically, it is bad policy. It is destructive to families.

Frazier said that I was missing the more basic issue, however: those who do get assistance get almost nothing. A penniless family of four in Alabama receives $147 a month on which to raise children. On top of that, they may get up to $264 monthly for food stamps. Their combined income of just over $400 would not bring them even halfway to the federal poverty level. Alabama assistance, he pointed out, ranked next to last among states in the nation.

I had quit taking notes. My head was full of figures and my body grew tense with growing anger. I had naively thought that by telling the Commissioner about this particular father I might somehow help him and the many like him. Instead, not only was this not going to happen, but Dr. Frazier was telling me things were even worse than I realized. Frustrated, I thanked him for his testimony and candor and called the next witness.

The anticipated relief was not forthcoming. Many of the stories were tragic, which was the term one of the witnesses used to describe what she sees. Nita Morrison, an employee of a community service agency in Tuscaloosa County, spoke of the "tragedy I see across my desk every day." She provided several examples, including the young man who had stopped by her office on the way home from his hospital dialysis treatment. The man and his wife said they didn't have one bite in their refrigerator to give their three children that night. "I am dying," the man told her, "and I know it. While I'm dying it's a heartache to see my children going hungry and I can't do anything about it."

The man had come that morning to attend the public hearing and to talk with the visiting doctors about his circumstances. But listening to the tragic stories of others who were hungry led to his early departure. He told Nita that he found it all unbearable.

For the next two hours we listened to one story after another, each describing poverty, hunger, homelessness, and malnutrition in the state. I was suddenly jarred by the voice of a dignified elderly woman who introduced herself as Virginia Durr, representing Church Women United.

As she spoke, Bill Beardslee recognized her and whispered to me, "That's the lady who bailed Rosa Parks out of jail." Rosa Parks's refusal to move to the back of a Montgomery public bus had marked the beginning of the American Civil Rights Movement. White, wealthy, and dignified, Mrs. Durr spoke to us as if addressing a group of well-meaning but ignorant children. Her manner and tone seemed justified, I thought, since I had told the audience we had come to learn why there was hunger in Alabama. Virginia Durr knew why and minced few words in her explanation.

"Food stamps are not for the disadvantaged," she asserted. "They're for the wealthy. The food stamp program provides a guaranteed market for agricultural products. Helping the poor is a consequence of the program, not its real purpose." Straightforward and direct, Mrs. Durr's demeanor nevertheless conveyed a sense of impatience that we had not yet understood a fundamental truth: The system of public assistance in this country has never been aimed primarily at solving the needs of the poor. "Yankee doctors have been coming South for years now," she concluded. "And we appreciate your concern. But only political power will solve the problem you are here to learn about."

After the session was over, the press began to ask questions. What did we learn? How bad is hunger in Alabama? Is it worse or better than elsewhere?

I told them we didn't yet know the answer to all their questions, that we had come to learn. But I suggested that their colleagues who had reported two days before on the flurry of tornadoes had missed the real story. Several people died, I recalled, and the press reported the tragedy in banner headlines. Yet the increasing infant mortality rate in the state means that more babies die unnecessarily every three days in Alabama than all the people who lost their lives during the storm. Those dead babies, however, never make it into the newspapers.

3

Appalachian Mountains and Coastal Towns

L ESS THAN A MONTH after we left Alabama, my colleagues and I were on a plane heading fron Boston to Tennessee and then on to North Carolina.*

I was ready for this trip. Much of the acute pain of what we had seen and heard in Mississippi and Alabama had dissipated, and I was curious to see if things could possibly be as bad in the mid-Atlantic states to which we were going. In

---

* We would rendezvous with Arden Miller, Chairman of Maternal and Child Health at the University of North Carolina School of Public Health; David Satcher, President of Maharry Medical College in Nashville; Agnes Lattimer, Medical Director of Cook County Hospital in Chicago; Amos Christie, Chairman Emeritus of Pediatrics at the Vanderbilt School of Medicine; Jim Carter, Chairman of the Department of Nutrition at Tulane University School of Public Health; and Myron Wegman, Dean Emeritus of the University of Michigan School of Public Health. Rounding out our group in Tennessee were physicians Jim Perrin, Paul Zee, Tom Yeager, J. C. Walker and Patricia Woodall; in North Carolina, we were assisted by Bill Dow and Jim Dykes, Sam Katz and Evelyn Schmidt.

the 1960s, "Appalachia" had become synonymous with excruciating poverty, yet remarkable progress had come about through local and federal efforts. We wanted a first-hand view of present conditions.

Two weeks before departure, however, we nearly canceled the trip. I had been informed that Jesse Helms was making inquiries about our group and planned to ambush us in some way. Helms is the senior senator from North Carolina, a well-known political figure who promotes his right-wing agenda in many ways.

I had given my staff, Debby Allen and Judy dePontbriand, much discretion in scheduling our field visits, telling them only that we wanted to see many different states. I had laid down just two ground rules: keep us on a busy pace from morning to night (a decree the doctors regretted after many grueling sixteen-hour workdays), and keep us out of politics. The latter point was especially important. We knew enough about hunger to know that it can be increased or decreased by political decisions. But I knew we had to keep out of politics ourselves. We couldn't be perceived as being in anyone's camp, or affiliated with any one political party or ideological position. We would be doctors and fact finders, pure and simple, and would ignore those politicians who might choose to praise us or malign us.

When plans of a political attack were reported, however, I grew worried. Some of the North Carolina doctors working with our staff expected a vitriolic Helms diatribe, branding us as "outside agitators." I could envision a big scene with Helms berating us and our becoming mired in a controversy that would create interesting heat in the press but not much light on the problem of hunger.

I ordered plans for the trip to be put on hold while I laid out my concerns to several colleagues. Their advice was helpful, but conflicting. Finally, I presented the case against going at a meeting with our Harvard staff, and shared my fears that disputes might jeopardize our future work and deflect attention from the problem of hunger. Staff member John Kellogg considered my argument, then said, "Larry, I think you might be right about all those points. But I remember that you said we wouldn't embroil ourselves in politics. You said we wouldn't look left or right, but stick to our job. If we're going to do it, we ignore Helms and go straight ahead."

Ten days later we left.

"A Mother Hurts When She Can't Feed Her Kids"

As our plane descended through the clouds to Knoxville, I remembered a personal mission I had in Tennessee. My eleven-year-old son Alex was heavily into country music, particularly favoring Dolly Parton and Kenny Rogers; he had great personal plans for moving to Nashville himself one day. Alex had asked me to bring him a souvenir from the state, and, knowing how full our days would be with more serious matters, I jotted a note to remind myself to do so.

I was soon made to remember how many kids haven't the luxury to dream so easily about their futures. At our briefing session in Knoxville, we learned that poverty had been increasing steadily during recent years. Only one-fourth of the poor received welfare assistance, although an astonishing 80 percent of them were children, women, and elderly people. The statistics made an impression, particularly as I thought of the children.

David Starling, a minister in the little mountain town of Jellico, warned us to be skeptical of the official statistics. He said that unemployment in his area is 20 percent officially, but that in reality it was closer to three times that figure. The proud and strong-willed hill families didn't like to apply for unemployment benefits or talk with strangers about their plight. Reverend Starling said that well over half the customers in grocery stores rely on food stamps, but that even so, most of the population "is falling through cracks in the safety net."

Our foray into the hills of Appalachia would soon render almost meaningless the statistics we had read in briefing books and staff papers. The people would remain in my memory long after the numbers had vanished.

I divided our team of doctors into three groups as we separated to spend two days in the hills of Tennessee with our local guides. These volunteers were church women and family physicians whose assistance was particularly helpful in the back roads and hidden "hollers" of the Appalachian Mountains.

The little winding road which took us into Jellico was a welcome sight. I had not wanted to stay behind in Knoxville with the team of colleagues I left there; I had never seen these mountain communities and longed to learn what the people in them are like and how they live. That opportunity was quickly provided by the director of the Crazy Quilt Friendship Center, who had invited us to meet with local women who convened there daily to eat, socialize, and sew quilts that are later sold in the cities.

The Center provides emergency food to people in the area. I talked with a family of six; the parents had just come back from Chicago, where the father unsuccessfully had tried to find a job. He had a serious back injury that limited his employment options, but was not qualified for SSI (disability insurance) for some reason. The family had applied for food stamps but was told that they could not expect any help for at least a month. Because he could not afford to see a doctor, the father could never obtain medical proof of his disability. Neither, therefore, could the family afford the surgery he needed on his back. As we talked with the man and wife it became obvious their entire life was a Catch-22. Doing one thing depended upon doing another, which they were unable to do for reasons they didn't control. Someone looking at the family as a statistic might conclude the father is lazy, because he wasn't supporting the family; I looked and saw a proud man being beaten down.

Twenty-seven-year-old Mickey sat nearby and had over-heard a bit of our conversation. The mother of three, she and her husband lived in a trailer in the hills. The loss of all her upper teeth made it difficult to understand her as she ex-plained that mealtime in the hills consisted mainly of spa-ghetti. "My husband's been lookin' for work a long time," she explained. "He got a job makin' $89 a week, but that made them cut off our welfare and Medicaid." This family was fur-ther ahead when he didn't work, but that hardly seemed to matter. The father's pride kept him on the job, although he risked certain financial catastrophe if a serious illness were to strike.

As we made small talk, Mickey confided that her husband had lived away for two years so his family could qualify for public assistance to help their children. My mind briefly flashed back to the father I met in Montgomery the previous month who had to do the same thing. Mickey said her children had often asked when their daddy would return, and she would have to explain that if he came back there would be less money to live on. It was hard, she said tearfully: "A mother hurts when she can't feed her kids."

Nutritionist Margaret LeBien told us that many parents in the Jellico area cannot feed their children. She had recently completed a market survey, costing the price of nutritionally balanced, low-cost meals at nearby markets. LeBien calcu-lated that adequate nutrition in mountain towns cost ninety cents per person per meal due to higher food transportation costs. In comparison, the average food stamp benefit was forty-six cents per meal, about half what was needed to meet nu-tritional standards. "There is just no way a family can stay healthy on a food-stamp budget," LeBien said.

LeBien was more than a little angry as she spoke. John Block, the Secretary of Agriculture in Washington, had re-cently tried to blunt growing criticism about the woeful nu-tritional inadequacy of food stamps by living with his family on a food-stamp budget for a week. He proclaimed the diet satisfactory. I had followed the story in the news, watching Block and his wife arrive at a District of Columbia market in their chauffeur-driven limousine with a shopping list in hand. The press followed behind as Mrs. Block, assisted by her husband, picked previously selected items from the shelves. The smiling couple passed through the checkout line to announce that they had bought groceries for a week and did not run over their budget. I was repelled at this example of government-by-publicity-stunt. Nutritionists within Block's own Department had concluded that while food stamps can tide a family over on a short-term basis, for the longer term they are inadequate. A family living within the food-stamp budget would inevitably become malnourished.

LeBien made the same point: "Any of us who are healthy could live on food stamps for a month or two. But if you're a child, or if you live on food stamps for a year or so, you're in trouble. You'll stay alive, but you will starve your body of adequate nutrients."

Later that day we saw little children whose bodies were being starved. Tilda Kemplin, director of the White Oak Mountain Day Care Center, reported that many of her children "are not up to snuff. They come in like little buds," she said, "with potential but not enough to blossom." After a few weeks at the Center, which provides two meals a day, they bloom. She proudly serves sixty children, but worries about the children in the mountains whom she knows are getting no help. Tilda discreetly pointed to a mother standing nearby and murmured that the woman had two girls she'd like to enroll in the Center. The father has had three heart attacks and brings in just over $300 monthly. "I visited them recently," Tilda said. "Their refrigerator was empty, and they had eaten nearly a hundred pounds of potatoes that month." But there are no places available in the program.

I wouldn't know it until later, but my first of only a few encounters with biased members of the press would begin that day. As Tilda and I talked a local UPI reporter listened.

As we concluded our conversation the young man asked if he could interview me, and I excused myself for several minutes to speak with him. A pencil behind his ear and another in hand to record my words, the young man acted brash and in charge. "Well, Dr. Brown," he began, "you said you came to the hills to learn about hunger, is that right?" I confirmed that statement, wondering how he could have missed it even though he had seemed very uninterested at a press briefing earlier in the day. "Well," he continued, "have you seen a hungry person yet?"

The reporter knew the answer to his own question. He had been with me for only a few minutes and knew we had made no home visits and that none of the doctors had examined people. We had heard much evidence of hunger at the Day Care Center; Tilda Kemplin's description of the area was overwhelming. But I had to say that I had not yet seen a hungry person that day.

The reporter left our group as we departed for home visits in the hills to see the families whose children need Tilda Kemplin's day-care program. But it would not be the last we would hear from him. The next day he wrote an article in which he alleged that I admitted having exaggerated the extent of poverty in America. Not only had I made no such "admission," but the subject of poverty itself had never been raised during our three-minute conversation. We had talked only about hunger.

It was of only slight consolation that a Tennessee physician traveling with us found that he, too, was quoted by the same reporter as saying things he never really said. Apparently the reporter had an axe to grind, and we were the tools chosen for the task. Had he stayed with us for the day he would have had the experience of seeing hunger at close range.

"It's Like Having Black Lung Disease"

Our first home visit that day was like looking at a book of Depression-year photographs and having them suddenly come to life. A tiny dirt road angled up a hill, past a rusting plow set against a group of small trees. At the top of the hill the road turned right, giving us a clear view of the homestead. It would have been the perfect picture for the cover of a *Life* magazine spread on American poverty in 1930. The house was wood, all wood, old and weathered by the elements. The roof sagged in the middle. A skinny dog came out from beneath the porch to inspect the visitors, only to retreat to sit beside an old washing machine.

The family—a husband, wife, and eight children—was milling about outside when we drove up with our local guide. The parents' faces looked like those I had seen a hundred times in pictures of Dust Bowl families migrating across America in the 1930s: long and lined, with hollow cheeks and prominent bones. A former miner, the forty-seven-year-old man was permanently disabled from black lung disease, a lasting imprint of years spent working beneath the surface of the hills nearby. The compensation for his condition was $300 a month in SSI disability assistance, supplemented by nearly the same amount in food stamps. This was the sole income for a family of ten, for food and rent for their dilapidated dwelling.

We talked for several minutes with the parents while the children gathered to listen. I was afraid that the weakened front porch might give way under the weight of the occupants, bringing a tangled mass of parents, children, and visiting doctors to a common landing spot beneath the structure. Trying not to be rude, I broke off the conversation to ask if we could go in. The house consisted of three rooms, with some makeshift furnishings. The refrigerator was ample in size, but inside there were only three biscuits, a stick of butter, and some frozen bones. As I closed the door of the freezer I turned to face the lens of a television camera that had recorded my inspection. Momentarily, I paused to wish that the young reporter who had badgered me about finding hungry people in the area had seen the paltry makings of a meal for ten people.

In the bedroom, Dr. Amos Christie was talking with the mother, who held a baby in her lap. Amos, in his seventies, had been in these hills many times during his tenure as chairman of the pediatrics department at Vanderbilt Medical School in Nashville. Now retired, Amos responded eagerly to my request for assistance and joined us on our venture to look into the living conditions of the hill people he served for so many years in the clinics he had established.

Immediately I knew why Amos was talking with the mother. The baby she held in her lap had Down's Syndrome, a form of mental retardation frequently associated with advanced maternal age. The mother seemed oblivious to the disability, telling Amos that this baby "jist ain't quite like the other 'uns was." Reportedly she had never received medical care for the child, whose condition was apparent to any health professional and to many lay persons. Gently, in low tones, the old pediatrician talked with the mother; I left the room to allow the privacy that seemed warranted by the moment.

Two of the other children, skinny and small for their ages, seemed to be in trouble. Pediatrician Tom Yeager held one, inconspicuously examining his limbs and stomach as he talked with the child. In answer to Tom's question, the four-year-old described what he had eaten that day. I moved near the father to engage him in conversation. The children were hungry, he acknowledged, but he wasn't quite sure what they would eat that evening. He mentioned nothing about his own needs, expressing concern only about the children he was trying to raise.

Next we drove a short distance to the Clear Fork Clinic. Amos had been instrumental in its creation. Over the years he had visited the clinic to check on the development of young physicians whom he had trained, some of whom moved on to practice in the mountains. Dr. J. C. Walker greeted Amos warmly and invited us in while he continued examining patients in the facility's tiny cubicles. "There aren't any problems in these mountains that new jobs wouldn't solve," he informed us. "Living on a fixed income here is like having black lung disease," he added, letting us draw the analogy of a slow death overtaking its victims.

The Clinic's administrator, Shirley Parker, described the hunger faced by their patients and called in the physician's assistant to give the results of a recently conducted growth study. The study had disclosed that twenty-two percent of the children examined were below the tenth percentile in height; I explained to the reporter next to me that we would normally expect only ten percent of the children to be in that growth category. This meant that more than twice the normal number of children examined by the clinic were short for their ages, an outcome known to relate to inadequate nutritional intake.

As the reporters asked questions I noticed an extremely thin girl observing the interview. I judged the child to be about seven, and I moved nearby to talk with her mother. As I accompanied them into Dr. Walker's examining room to ask him to look at the child, the parent confessed that Betty was well beyond nine. Dr. Walker reported that her slight build and lack of tissue in the upper arms was not uncommon for children in that area. He conducted appropriate blood work even though we both knew that the child almost certainly was anemic.

Throughout the afternoon my colleagues and I scoured the tiny towns in the region. In East Jackson Jim Carter teamed up with Paul Zee, the Chief of Nutrition at St. Jude's Hospital in Memphis, an institution whose name has become synonymous with its chief benefactor, actor Danny Thomas. Stopping at Hope Church, Jim and Paul learned of a growing number of "car families" in the area. "We see them every day," noted Mary Tyler, who directs a social service program. "They have no houses, just live in their cars."

These Americans do not fit easily into stereotypes about the poor. Most of them are white, about three-fourths of them under the age of fifteen. "They live in their car while their parents drive about searching for work. Except for us," Mary reported, "they have nowhere else to eat. I mean nowhere!"

"In a funny way it hits the men the hardest," injected Reverend Davis, pastor of Hope Church. "The stress leads to emotional depression, family squabbles. Often it's divorce. Breaks 'em right apart."

"People Here Want Jobs"

Our visits to homes that day ended early enough to permit time for the return trip to Knoxville, where a public hearing had been scheduled that evening. By the time we arrived the church was packed with people. One of the first witnesses was Robert Wilson, an employee of the city in the planning department. "The government's role in assuring that people are fed," he said, "should be like assuring that the public has water to drink. It's ironic that we accept government responsibility for providing water but not food," he concluded.

Lawrence Ritchie, a local physician, called our attention to the injustice of hunger in the region. "We uphold freedom in our nation, but is not poverty a form of slavery? Isn't it exploitation of people for economic gain?" Karen Braswell, a native who had been laid off work and was now without food, elaborated. "Most of us have lived here all our lives," she began. "But our land is owned by big corporations. We can't develop the land where we live, not even for garden plots." As she spoke I recalled the words of Virginia Durr in Alabama: "You doctors can't separate the problem of hunger from political power."

The testimony of the hungry generally was more simple

and straightforward. Nettie Ballinger stepped to the front of the hall to say that food stamps are the sole source of income for herself and her unemployed husband. "I know I'm fat," she acknowledged, "but we're also hungry. The doctor says I have vitamin deficiencies, but we can't afford anything but cheap, filling food."

Joanne Edmonds described herself as a single parent whose marriage ended after a serious car accident. Formerly middle-class, according to her account, she became poor and was hungry until she was able to get food stamps. "They made the difference in my life . . ." she began as her voice cracked and she sought to regain her composure. She was followed by Virginia Carter, who had come to tell us that her family is not hungry, but that people in her neighborhood regularly collect cans to sell to buy food. "People here want jobs," she added.

The parade of residents describing the pervasiveness of hunger was interrupted periodically by public officials and health professionals who knew the problem as observers rather than as victims. Doug Coulter reported that the mayor had become so concerned by growing hunger that he had developed a mechanism to coordinate emergency food assistance and had expanded the Knoxville school breakfast program. Attorney Helen Trout observed that minimum-wage jobs are advertised in the local paper and hundreds of people line up to apply. "Unemployment," she added, "is much higher than official government statistics report."

Maynard Trailer, a public health professor at the University of Tennessee, estimated that hunger in the region is not yet as bad as it was in the early 1960s, but "the problem has definitely increased over the last several years." Data provided by ministers and soup kitchen workers supported his analysis. Most of the facilities in the area were showing increases of up to 200 percent each year in the numbers of people seeking emergency food assistance.

Reverend Jim Sessions, a United Methodist minister, told

us that he and his colleagues work throughout Appalachia, and "the hunger and malnutrition we see is a real problem—a daily problem." His observation seemed to tally with what we had seen and heard. We had been in the area only a short time, but had seen enough to let us know that a significant segment of citizens in this part of the nation was experiencing deprivation of shocking proportions. We not only found the "hungry person" the young reporter had asked me about, but many of them. And those we had not seen directly we saw through the eyes of the people who know.

"I SEE THE EMPTY REFRIGERATORS"

Less than twelve hours later we were in Nashville, where Mayor Robert Fulton welcomed us to the city. In a personal aside the Mayor confessed that he no longer goes to oversee the distribution of surplus cheese and butter. "I run into people I went to school with. They feel embarrassed when they see me," he told me. Noting that a portion of the middle class in his city had recently fallen into poverty, Fulton requested that we "Please tell Mr. Meese and the White House that there is hunger in America."

According to the medical staff of the city's General Hospital where we went next, the Mayor had cause for concern. Dr. Joseph McLaughlin, director of the maternal and infant care program, reported that the incidence of low-birth-weight babies (infants with weight under five-and-a-half pounds) had increased 16 percent since 1981. These infants are much more likely to die during their first year of life. For several years, Dr. McLaughlin explained, the rate of low birth weights had been declining, and the medical staff felt good about their progress. Then, starting in 1981, the rate began to increase again.

Nutritionist Denise Griffin said the increase was not entirely unexpected, given the difficulties poor people in the area were having. According to their recent patient survey, more than a third of all patients run out of food before the end of each month. Griffin sees a lot of nutritional deficiencies among her clients. "We're particularly concerned about the number of pregnant women who are losing weight during their pregnancies," she said. "One woman had recently lost three pounds, so we sent out a nutritionist to her home. We found that the family had no food in the house, and food stamps would not arrive for another week." It was common, Griffin reported, for pregnant women to be without food, and lack of food for them meant lack of adequate nutrition for the babies they carry.

After leaving the hospital we visited day-care centers and homes in the city. We learned that once they leave the hospital, babies may continue to be at risk. Mrs. Otis, director of a small day-care program in her home, said that the children for whom she cares get little to eat other than what she can provide them. "Previously we just had to worry about the babies over the weekends, but now some get nothing to eat, even at night." Mrs. Mapole, who also runs a small program in her own home, sees children under one year of age coming in hungry. "That baby over there," she gestured, "just ate three portions for breakfast; he gets little to eat over the weekend and comes in here almost starved." Mrs. Mapole quickly added, "The parents aren't really wasting their money, they just don't have it. I go in their homes and see the empty refrigerators. I see what's on the tables," she concluded, "you can't tell me things aren't getting worse."

We saw the empty tables too and talked with the mothers trying to feed their families. As we visited with Margaret Brown and her neighbors she described her family's diet: "We eat mainly potatoes and beans, things to fill us up. Food stamps don't last, so we have to be careful about eating more expensive things like meat or fruit. Mostly potatoes and beans," she repeated. Another woman joined the conversation to say that her family doesn't get vegetables after the first of the month. "My husband and kids call our food 'reruns' 'cause it's the same every day. I wish I could do better, but the filling stuff stretches further."

A self-assured mother spoke up as if something her neighbor said had clicked in her mind. "I go to the market, plan a list, get what I think my family should have, then have to return half the items because food stamps don't last." She lives on $127 a month for herself and two children. Then, as if to speak for the several women who had agreed to talk with us, she added: "This is not the way we want to raise our children. People should work; welfare isn't the answer. But we have to have jobs and day care. If you hate welfare like we do, come up with a workable plan. Get us some jobs!"

Laura MacAfee wants a job. This ninety-three-year-old woman lives with her retired son in a small house on a dirt road outside Nashville. Their combined income from social security and disability is $315 monthly, plus another $28 in food stamps. "We live kinda hard," Laura acknowledged as I looked in the kitchen to find white beans and potatoes, "but we ain't hungry." But Laura's thin body and dietary intake belied her statement. When I pursued the matter she conceded that there were times when they had nothing to eat. "I been thinkin'," she answered, "that maybe I could get myself a job to help make things stretch." Laura's plight was not unusual in the experience of a public health nurse whose name I never learned. No starvation, the nurse said, but more and more of her clients cannot buy the food they need. "Federal budget cuts limit the options, even for my little old ladies in the housing projects."

Not all of the residents were little old ladies. Twenty-one-year-old Cathy Lucas' husband is quadriplegic, the result of damage suffered at the time of an arteriogram. Their total income is almost $250, $139 in food stamps, the rest in disability. When he had first applied for SSI disability insurance, his claim was denied; the worker, operating under stricter federal rules, deemed that Mr. Lucas was employable. It took two months to get that decision reversed. Meanwhile, Cathy had cut down on the number of meals she and her husband ate from two to one a day. His condition required a special diet, one she couldn't possibly prepare; meanwhile he developed an ulcer.

The depression engendered by home visits was alleviated slightly by conversations at two government offices. We asked Marc Overlook of the Tennessee Department of Human Services why so many of the needy people we had seen get no food stamps. His response was that new, more stringent federal regulations have led to more red tape. It was the same answer we had heard in Mississippi and Alabama. "When burdensome requirements are placed on families trying to hold on, they frequently cannot comply," he said. Overlook described the insidious nature of the new regulations. "We recently had to deny food stamps to a family that had no income whatsoever. They lost their apartment and someone let them move into his home on a temporary basis. But the regulations require us to treat the good Samaritan's income as if it was the income of the applicant family. We knew it was not their income, but Washington tied our hands. God knows what'll happen to these poor people."

In nearby Gallatin County, legal services attorney Kathy Skaggs represents other families like this one. She described a vicious circle of mean-spirited rules and regulations that prevent people from getting the help they need and deserve. "The Washington administration is so suspicious of poor people that they set up regulations and go back even years trying to 'catch' those who make twenty-nine cents too much." One client, a handicapped woman, got a food stamp termination notice because she had received $39 too much. Subsequent investigation showed that the error had been made by the agency threatening to cut her off. Skaggs was able to help this client, but not a lot of those she knows. The legal services budget had been cut back in the area, and fewer attorneys now assist the poor.

Tennessee made a strong impression on me and my colleagues as we prepared to leave. A beautiful and varied state, its rural areas and cities are home for thousands of families who are hardly making it. The state has no general assistance program and doesn't provide public assistance if the father is in the home. This means that the main assistance program is food stamps, which constitutes the tattered safety net that exists in the state. And that program is reaching fewer and fewer people because of hostile federal regulations. The people see it, doctors and nurses see it, and so do the other professionals who try to respond to the malnutrition and hunger that come as a result.

"We all look at statistics," commented Dr. Tom Yeager, "but in the last three days I just saw people, people with a lot of pride who had trouble even admitting their problems. The statistics we read about are people's lives." Tom's feelings were shared by Myron Wegman, an annual contributor to health and medical journals on the subject of infant mortality. Myron observed that we are saving more and more high-risk babies through advanced medical technology, but not feeding many of them enough to reach their full potential. "I hate to suggest it," he added, "but with all the waste in the Pentagon I wouldn't mind 'wasting' a little bit of food for these kids."

"ACROSS THE GREAT SMOKIES"

The Great Smoky Mountains form the border between Tennessee and North Carolina, our next destination. But just as the scenic beauty of the land does not stop at the border dividing the states, neither does the problem that prompted our trip. Near the border I stopped the car, informing my colleagues that I needed to select several choice Tennessee rocks for my son's collection; fortunately, someone had said something that reminded me of the request Alex had made before I left Boston.

North Carolina is known for its universities and high-technology industries, epitomized by the "Research Triangle" area that encompasses Raleigh, Durham, and Chapel Hill. I had been in the state only a year before lecturing to a group of public health students whose professor had been a student of mine at Harvard. On that trip I had seen the glittery side of the state; now I would see the poor whose lives are overshadowed by the centers of productivity and learning.

A state with varied terrain, North Carolina has all manner of poverty: poor white hill people, black families living in inner cities, migrant camps whose inhabitants are among the most oppressed and downtrodden in the nation, and American Indians. Eighteen percent of the state was already living in poverty at the time of our visit, including 415,000 children—and it was getting worse.

Poverty is not the only thing increasing in North Carolina. Hunger is increasing dramatically, as is infant mortality. In Madison County, 20 percent of the children served by the WIC supplemental feeding program are anemic; in Durham the figure is over 60 percent. And it's not just the children who suffer. Durham home-health nurse Alice Walker had detected health deficiencies in three-fourths of the 400 elderly patients for whom she cares.

Our first glimpse of hunger came in the lush rolling mountains surrounding Asheville at the western end of the state bordering Tennessee. This community of 53,000 is home of the Grove Street Senior Citizens' Center run by Mrs. MacDaniels. As several doctors entered the hall where cheese and butter distribution takes place, the lights of the television crew covering our visit drew the attention of the dozens of old people who had come for food. We dispersed to talk with guests and staff.

I sat next to Mrs. Jarrett, an elderly woman who used a cane to walk. Now sitting in a metal folding chair, she shifted uncomfortably to ease the pain in her joints. "I used to get cheese and butter," she said, "but now I have to fill out these forms to prove I'm not a cheat." The old woman was the target of new federal procedures that were making it harder for elderly clients to qualify. Those who come every few months for surplus government cheese now had to complete elaborate verification requirements to "prove" their eligibility. It seemed like an onerous requirement to receive a five-pound block of cheese, but government leaders wanted to get tough on waste.

Once certified eligible, the elderly recipient is supposed to drive in to pick up the cheese. If they have no car, they can take the bus. Except for the Mrs. Jarretts of the community, that is, who cannot walk. But the government regulations requiring the more cumbersome procedures don't seem to take them into account.

Virginia Eldreth, administrator of the local food stamp office, complained that Washington "changes procedures and requirements every time we distribute cheese and butter; they make it less accessible to the poor." She suggested that the elderly should be treated differently so they would not have to go through all the red tape. Why just for the elderly, I asked, wondering why it is that we categorize people by age, race, and marital status as a way to determine who is most deserving. "Well, maybe for the others, too," she answered, "it may cause less stigma, too."

I could see what she meant about the stigma. The Asheville food stamp office is not an inviting facility to visit, whether you are a visiting doctor or a citizen seeking some short-term assistance when your family is down on its luck. Staring me in the face as I entered was a newspaper account of food stamp fraud, the story of a woman who was being prosecuted for receiving more stamps than she was eligible for. I had been to the office of the Internal Revenue Service in Boston only a couple of months before to pick up tax forms, and I thought how odd it would have been to be greeted by a newsclip on IRS fraud. It's illegal to cheat the government, but taxpayers are not harassed by impolite and intimidating signs in public offices.

Adorning the walls along the narrow corridor back to Mrs. Eldreth's office were red-and-white signs prominently displayed for all to see. "WARNING," they shouted in bold letters, "we prosecute food stamp recipients for intentionally making false statements . . ." Small letters at the bottom of the warning signs added a perverse notice of non-discrimination: "Program violators will be prosecuted without regard to race, color, national origin, age, sex, handicap, political beliefs or religion."

Suppressing an urge to comment on this unique manifestation of social justice, I asked Mrs. Eldreth if people would not find the signs discouraging. "Yes, definitely," she admitted, acknowledging that the office decorations may intimidate perfectly honest people when they are already in a vulnerable state. She then recounted for us the case of an old lady who had recently come in to apply for food stamps on the persistent advice of her grown daughter. "Seeing the old lady's hand shake vigorously while she filled out the numerous application forms, our food stamp worker was shocked to learn that her problem was not due to a lack of fine motor coordination. She had read the fraud warning signs and was fearful that she would make a mistake on her application and be thrown in jail." It was quite a story, but Jim Carter observed that Eldreth is not the problem. "She's just following orders from Washington," he mused. "You know, sort of like the Nuremberg trials."

We learned that the county was engaged in a food-stamp-fraud campaign. Undercover agents were sent out to try to sell stamps to unsuspecting citizens. The arrests of "cheaters" were sensationalized in the local paper, and prosecution followed. It was an official effort to try to blow the issue of fraud all out of proportion.

That night I recalled the issue of intimidating potential recipients under the guise of ending fraud. "Why did we find it in Asheville, North Carolina, and not in Tennessee or Maine?" I asked one of my colleagues. "Come on, Larry," he said half-jokingly, "surely you've heard of Jesse Helms?" I recalled how I had almost canceled the entire field trip because of the perceived threats of this same man, and my empathy for Mrs. Eldreth quickened.

Later that afternoon two of us went with our guide to conduct several home visits in the nearby town of Black Mountain, leaving our colleagues to interview families in other towns. The deteriorating home of the Fox family was relatively isolated and, despite its state of repair, appealing to the eye as we drove up a side road to the front door.

It seemed fateful to make this home visit following our meeting in the food stamp office that scared its clients. With a wife and two preschool children, Mr. Fox was failing as a self-employed lawn mower repairman, but had been too proud to apply for food stamps. For several months his wife pleaded with him to allow her to apply; many times they had no food in the house. When they were luckier, they lived on only one meal a day, even when Mrs. Fox was pregnant.

Their daughter had been born during better times and weighed seven pounds at birth; the little boy, born during days of unemployment, was less fortunate. At birth, he weighed three pounds, one ounce. He picked up weight substantially once the father applied for food stamps, but did not talk in complete sentences at the age of three. Why, I asked the parents, trying to look at neither of them in particular, did you wait so long to go for food stamps? "It's just in my nature," Mr. Fox responded slowly, studying a paint splotch on the living room floor. Thirty seconds went by before his wife decided to give her own version of what clearly must have led to family tension: "He heard that food stamp people was cheats and he was too proud to be one of 'em."

Down the road from the Foxes lived Mrs. Herbert, who certainly didn't look hungry. An obese mother of a five-year-old son and a daughter about seven, half her $381 monthly income was from food stamps. Her children often went without milk for more than a week's time. I opened the refrigerator to find only surplus government cheese. The reporter accompanying us eyed the woman, as if to wonder how a fat person could be hungry. It is a common misperception among non-medical people that obesity means one eats too much. In one sense, of course, that is true, but it is not an honest explanation. As I questioned Mrs. Herbert about the family's dietary patterns, I learned that she had a pretty good idea of proper nutrition, but could not afford high-quality fruits and vegetables. "All I can afford is the things that'll fill up me and my kids," she confessed. They were overweight, but they were also hungry.

What we and our colleagues saw that day in the Asheville area belied the beauty and tranquility of the resort region. We found hunger, and we learned that local doctors are seeing more seriously ill children. We found the federal food stamp program weakened by politically motivated rhetoric against the poor. More people were hungry, but fewer were getting help. The rolling hills of western North Carolina, we learned, harbor a dark secret, one we had uncovered before leaving for an Indian community in Halifax County to the east.

"UNOFFICIAL INDIANS AND CRIMINAL FAMILIES"

On the door of the Haliwa-Saponi Tribal Council office a sign announced that food co-op prices had been slashed. One could now purchase oatmeal for 88¢, beans for 33¢, and Fruit Loops for $1.09. I ignored my curiosity about the strange mixture of items as Meshelia Richardson met us at the door.

The Saponi and Tutelo tribes, she told us, are comprised of about two thousand people who have no federal recognition as "official Indians." I wondered what that governmental distinction meant. Were they "unofficial Indians," or just plain Americans? I concluded from her disgression that not being an "official Indian" means not being under the jurisdiction of the federal Bureau of Indian Affairs. From the books I had read about the Bureau's treatment of Indian tribes, I concluded it may be better to be "unofficial." I would learn that I was wrong.

"Richardson" seemed to be the "Brown" or "Jones" of the Indian tribes, as this was also the name of the woman who operated the day-care center nearby. I left the company of the two pediatricians who were with me to sit next to Regina, a five-year-old who looked no more than three-and-a-half. Her plate was entirely empty; I envisioned its contents in her tiny tummy. Mrs. Richardson said, "Regina was quite listless when she first entered the program, but she's grown noticeably. Her speech was not good when she came in, but now it's better." Most of the families in the area are poor, Mrs. Richardson noted, and many children don't get enough to eat. As we talked, Jim Dykes examined several of the children. A few showed signs of possible malnutrition: pale lips and nails, poor teeth and apparent growth retardation.

We soon departed to make home visits to Indian families in the area. Our first stop was a tiny shack with two rooms and no toilet. The shack housed two parents and their four children, ages three and under, including a two-week-old infant. The father had been unemployed for four months, during which time their sole income was $300 in food stamps. The baby lay on a bed, flies all over her face. An empty plastic bottle with a blue top lay by her side as she cried. In the refrigerator were eight eggs, some government cheese, and dry cereal. There was no milk.

"How long have you been without milk for the babies?" I asked.

"About a week," the mother replied.

"What did you give the children for breakfast today?"

"Bologna. It's gone now," she answered.

"What did you have for lunch?"

"No lunch," she murmured.

One of the doctors nudged me to come see the two-year-old, a cute little boy whose sole garment was a dirty T-shirt.

The pediatrician bent over to stroke his orange hair and, referring to the discoloration, whispered, "Talk about malnutrition."

In the car I said to the reporter, "Now that's a criminal family."

"What?"

"Yes. They're violating federal laws and engaging in welfare fraud," I added with a smile. "I know because the family has no cash income. They couldn't pay their twenty-dollar rent or their light bill unless they traded their food stamp coupons for money. It's illegal even to buy sanitary napkins or bathroom supplies with the food stamps."

The reporter was skeptical and asked how I could be so certain they had traded their stamps for money to pay expenses.

"Let's go back in and ask," I said, half as a dare.

We returned to the house and I spoke with the mother.

"Ma'am, how many of your food stamps do you have to sell to get the cash you need each month?"

In a matter-of-fact tone, with no hesitation, she answered, "I'm not really sure, my husband takes care of that."

At that we left. In the car we discussed the question of welfare fraud and wondered how many families were sacrificing milk for their children, in order to pay rent or utility bills. We all agreed that the trade-offs forced upon the poor are shameful.

The Tribal Council social worker had tried to enroll the three older children in the day-care program, but no slots were open. Why, asked Jim Dykes, could they not be accepted, given their obvious physical conditions? "There are a lot of children like them," the social worker responded, "you just saw one family." To respond to this need, she added, the Tribal Council had tried to open a Head Start program. Their application had been rejected by the federal government.

As we drove on, Jim spotted a woman standing between two wooden shacks at the side of the road and asked our driver to stop the car. Three of us walked toward her, obviously taking the woman by surprise as very few people travel along her road. As we approached, her smile broadened and she began to wave. "Doctor," she called out, recognizing Jim as the doctor who cares for two of her children. "Please come in." Inside, we chatted while her children played on the floor.

"Do you folks have a problem getting food?" Jim asked.

"Well, I suppose. We do run out a lot. We just don't make enough."

Back in the car I asked Jim how long he had known the family.

"It's not how long, but how well," he said. "I've been seeing the children in my clinic for some time. A while ago I diagnosed both of them as failing to grow normally. I'm embarrassed to say that I never went to their home to find out why they weren't developing. Now I know."

"HE BEGGED FOR JOBS AND FOOD"

In Roanoke Rapids the Union Mission feeds some sixty people a day. Reverend Jones, a man who looks more like a mechanic than a minister, reported that the store-front facility is getting more requests for food from elderly people and young families. Did he ever see families coming in to say that their children have no food? we inquired. "Yeah, many times. I could fill the Mission with them," he replied, adding that he was trying to open a soup kitchen because there are so many of them.

Living behind the mission in a condemned apartment the size of a large lean-to, we met elderly Georgiana Jones. The recipient of $313 in monthly disability assistance and $13 in food stamps, she had been put on a special high-fiber diet by a doctor, but she could not afford the higher-priced foods. The stove in her dwelling showed the remains of her meal for the day, a hot sausage and bread.

Three or four blocks away, eighty-year-old Mrs. Freeman

sat on the porch of her wooden shack-like home, surrounded by three friends. One turned out to be a disabled son who lives with her, surviving on $313 monthly in social security benefits. No food stamps. The four figures were in mourning for Mrs. Freeman's forty-eight-year-old son who had suddenly died the past Sunday "while he was a sittin' right there in that chair." The old lady had no idea what caused her son's death. Later the local guide accompanying us around the area confided that the man had begged a lot in the town. "He begged mostly for jobs but sometimes for food," he elaborated. Whatever the cause of death, his life couldn't have been a happy one. He lived and died in a house with no running water, no toilet, and no outhouse, a dwelling that was still home to his elderly mother and his brother.

Back in Durham we met with Dan Hudgins, an earnest and straightforward professional who directs the Durham County Department of Social Services. Dan recounted recent events in the state to help us gain perspective. "Normally," he pointed out, "food stamp participation increases during times of economic recession in order to help the growing number of people who need it. Between 1981 and 1983, poverty went up 42 percent in North Carolina. But food stamp assistance, instead of going up, actually went down. Down by about 100,000 people. As a result, hunger became serious, and emergency programs sprang up in the area to try to put their collective fingers in the Durham dike."

Sister Helen is one of the local dike repairers. The Urban Ministry, a collective endeavor of several religious denominations, administers unto the victims of the poor economy and faltering food stamp program. Sister Helen said there are two problems most of the families have: the first is that many bureaucratic barriers prevent them from getting food stamps; the other is that food stamps don't last out the month anyway. As a consequence, her program serves large numbers of families with small children who have nothing to eat. That morning, for example, she had seen a family with five children, a family that couldn't get food stamps because they lacked some document needed to prove their eligibility. The mother is working, the father is in the hospital, and the seventeen-year-old son stays out of school to care for a preschool sister. Sister Helen was unashamed of her calmly expressed anger: "Poor families constantly are put in a position of being in crisis, always having to beg for food. Tell me why the richest country in the world puts 15 percent of the people in this state in a position of begging for food each month."

"Sometimes you wish the government would help," observed Frank VandenEyden in the office of Catholic Parish Outreach just down the street. Having fed over a thousand people a month for the past four months, most of them families, the small program was having to cut back on aid. Spending some $1,000 weekly, it was running out of funds. The demand had not trailed off after December, as the agency anticipated. "People have just kept coming, people who are out of work and hungry."

Wake County health department staff gathered to tell our visiting team of the hunger they see every day in their patients. Barbara Mann said that year-old children get removed from her WIC supplemental feeding program because they are in good health. Frequently the children return, anemic, because their parents haven't enough food. Only about half the children eligible for the program are served due to federal funding constraints. "People absolutely run out of food," she assured us as if we doubted her account.

The home health nurse corroborated the point, telling of the young mothers she sees in homes where there is no food in the house. Many of them dilute their baby's formula to try to make it last, a practice that leads to "water intoxication," which poses a serious threat to the infant.

Helen Cannon, a physician with the health department, said that her clinic had been seeing an increasing number of infants and small children suffering from failure to thrive, plus a number of infant deaths in cases where the birth weight was extremely low. Cannon pointed also to the pervasive emphasis on weeding out food stamp fraud, rather than trying to help the needy. "All the bad publicity from the politicians is making people reluctant to even try to get food stamps. And then we wonder why the infant mortality rate is so high."

Ginny Britt of the Samaritan Soup Kitchen said she was surprised that the undercover agents had found no one willing to buy the discounted black market food stamps. "People have to sell and buy stamps to survive in this area. The response of public officials to hunger is like the German response to the Holocaust. They say, 'We don't see it, we don't know.' "

The Holocaust analogy seemed a bit strong to me, but I reconsidered it as I listened to Al Deitch, a state official involved in efforts to alleviate hunger. North Carolina has no Medicaid program for children of intact families, he reported, nor does it provide welfare assistance when the father remains with the family. Day-care centers are full, and children come in hungry, especially on Mondays after a weekend with little food.

"Eleven hundred babies in the state die each year," according to Deitch, "making this one of the worst ten states in the nation insofar as infant deaths." Concluding his comments with a glance at his notes, he saw that he had overlooked one of his points. "We're 45th among the states in our level of public assistance. Families getting it and food stamps combined still live at 54 percent of the poverty level."

As we prepared to board our plane members of our group chatted, each in his way acknowledging that the hunger, poverty, and ill health we had seen in Tennessee and North Carolina had been extreme. Agnes Lattimer said that what she would remember most vividly was the farmworkers who picked fruit and vegetables but could not afford to buy that same produce in the store. Jim Carter pointed to the elderly black woman who had come to legal services with her ten-dollar monthly allotment of food stamps saying, "There must be some mistake." Another colleague said she would remem-

ber the hill people who paid one dollar and nine cents for a
can of tuna that cost sixty-nine cents in an affluent suburb.
We all would remember empty cupboards and refrigerators,
hunger that was obvious in homes of black, white, and Indian
families.

Sitting atop the poverty and hunger was a coating of government meanness: messages of intimidation, words of dem-
agoguery and denial. "In North Carolina," said Ed King, a
local church official, "one sometimes sees the far extreme of
the Protestant ethic, the notion that if someone is hurting
they deserve it. I have always thought that providing for the
public welfare is a guarantee of the United States Constitution.
But in North Carolina some politicians try to make that a bad
thing."

As I headed to the airport, I was glad that I had not let
Jesse Helms stand in the way of our field trip to North Carolina. But he stands in the way of many of the helpless people
we had seen. I thought of them as I recalled the words of a
young woman who approached me as I left for my flight: "I
think, Doctor, that it's not charity that is needed, but justice."

4

Dimmed Hopes in the
Sun Belt

THE SUMMER INTERLUDE before our scheduled trip to the Southwest helped to provide perspective on what we had seen in the ten states we had already visited. But there had been no respite for Danny Holley, whose death was front-page news in papers across the nation.

The eldest of three brothers and sisters, young Danny lived with his mother on an army base in Marino, California; his father was overseas. Life on the base was difficult, and his mother frequently confided to her oldest child that there was not enough food for the family. To help, thirteen-year-old Danny took it upon himself to collect cans and bottles for redemption, turning the money over to his mother to buy groceries. But the Holleys continued to go to bed hungry.

One night Danny got a rope, carefully tied it in knots, and hanged himself. He had left his mother a note, as if an explanation could somehow relieve the anguish she would feel. "If there is one less mouth to feed," the note said, "things will be better."

I followed the story throughout the summer of 1984, wondering if Danny's tragic death would somehow call public attention to the constantly escalating problems of hunger, homelessness, and poverty in the land. Yet little was said about Danny. President Reagan and former Vice President Mondale were locked in a heated election campaign, and the public was concerned with other issues. Danny Holley's life seemed to be one of those things that slips through the cracks of our national conscience.

"EVERY YEAR A FEW OLD PEOPLE STARVE TO DEATH"

As our plane approached Albuquerque, I peered out the small windows and gazed in awe at the rich earth tones of empty vastness encircling the city's urban sprawl. Red cliffs rise sharply from the desert soil, and the dry air gives the impression one can see forever. The beauty is unmistakable. Yet the very surroundings were to be an omen for what we would see during our visit to the Southwest: a land of extraordinary natural beauty masking the ugly man-made problems of poverty.

Fourteen physicians participated in our fieldwork in New Mexico and Texas. Some, like Naomi Kistin, Aaron Shirley, and Bill Beardslee, had been on trips earlier that spring, which enabled them to compare experiences in the Southwest with other regions. Others, like Joyce Lashoff, Dean of the School of Public Health at the University of California, Berkeley, and Stephen Berman, Chairman of Pediatrics and Adolescent Medicine at the University of Colorado in Denver, brought fresh perspectives from states we would not have time to investigate. A third group of physicians, including Judith Kitzes of the Albuquerque Area Indian Health Service, José Rodriguez from Clínica La Fe, in El

Paso, and Fernando Guerra, Medical Director of the Barrio Health Center in San Antonio, provided welcome, firsthand experience as medical practitioners and public health professionals in the Southwest.

At the airport we split up into separate teams. The hot, dry air assaulted our faces as Bill, Joyce, and Aaron climbed into waiting cars for their three-hour drive to Crownpoint, a small town on the Navajo Reservation at the state's border with Arizona. Rounding out their team was Dick Kozol, a physician who serves as director of the Checkerboard Area Health System in Cuba, New Mexico. Dick's experience in New Mexico, along with Judith's, proved invaluable for our understanding of the problems faced by Native Americans.

Miles of land stretched on either side of the highway as they sped toward the Navajo Reservation. It was, as they later recounted, an impressive landscape broken by mesas and buttes, yet virtually devoid of houses or people. "Water is everything here," Dick pointed out. "It determines the use of the land and where people live. The land that's been left for the Indians will support a little grazing, a small garden," he paused a moment and reflected, ". . . or maybe nothing at all."

The face of this land created the culture of the Navajo people, dictating that people live in relatively isolated extended-family homesites separated by miles of stark emptiness. The costs of gasoline and car maintenance put added economic strains on an already poor people. No more than fifteen hundred of the five thousand miles of roads on the reservation are paved. The huge distances are made longer by the endless ruts and bumps caused by the action of rain and sun. Only one-third of the houses have electricity; less than half have running water or plumbing.

As Dick briefed the team on the health and social problems they would encounter, the land's variegated hues swept by: red, brown, and tan dancing off the rock and sand, punctuated by dark green mesquite and piñion trees, and shaded by lighter greens from the ground cover and wildflowers. "Accidents are a leading cause of death," Dick reported. "Alcoholism and psychiatric disorders are common; so are nutritional deficiencies. Unemployment is high, listed at forty percent in some areas, but in reality probably even higher. There is little reason to expect that a significant number of new jobs can be created by the private sector."

The team's first stop was at Crownpoint, for a briefing led by home health nurse Harriet Evans, herself a Navajo. "Families around here are dependent on old pickup trucks for transportation," Evans said. "The children may spend four hours a day in schoolbuses going to and from school. The water they drink must be hauled to homes in drums. I drive throughout the area to deliver medicines and check on the elderly. A lot of times I try to make sure they get some food. Generally, they run out of food at the end of the month when the food stamps run out."

After the briefing, the doctors hopped into a van, driving off for house calls in the countryside. For an hour and a half they flew along back roads at breakneck speed, seeking out homes set far back in the desert-like countryside. They stopped at a hogan, a small, traditional octagonal Indian dwelling. Next door was a little house, bare of the amenities most of us associate with home. Peeking into the hut, Bill spied an old woman squatting on the dirt floor. Heat radiated from the stovepipe that ran through the center of the mud roof.

Speaking in a hushed tone to avoid alarming the woman, their local guide explained, "She's ninety-three years old and has diabetes and chronic illnesses. She just moved from the house of her son who has epileptic seizures. In Navajo culture someone with seizures is a witch, so they won't sleep under the same roof with him." The family's diet was composed largely of potatoes, squash, and corn, the nutritionist added. "They have no refrigeration, no fresh fruits or vegetables. They have no milk."

The team's next stop was in Window Rock, at the headquarters of the Tribal Administration. An aide to Peterson

Zah, head of the Navajo Nation, had come to emphasize the need for government-sponsored nutrition programs on the reservation. "The school lunch program is essential, as practically all the students qualify for the benefit. But some schools lack refrigerators and are therefore not eligible for the program. The feeding program for the elderly provides food for a significant portion of the elderly, but some of the congregate centers cannot pass sanitation inspection. . . . The food stamp program for the reservation is administered through three different states, while the Tribal Council has been able to get one contract for WIC. The amount of paperwork and bureaucracy involved in a program administered through three separate states is phenomenal." The doctors wondered why the federal government did not simplify the process, employing a single administration through the Bureau of Indian Affairs; obviously, that would be the most efficient way to get food stamps to the people. No one had an answer for Washington's rules.

More than a hundred miles away, my colleagues and I listened to a briefing session at the Roadrunner Food Bank in Albuquerque. We also were hearing about life in the Indian communities. As Ona Porter, a staff member on the Albuquerque Indian Health Board summarized, "Every year a few old people starve to death in the Indian communities. Most of the elderly are malnourished. At least one-third of the children have iron deficiencies. Nearly all the pregnant women are anemic and suffer vitamin deficiencies."

Dr. Fitzhugh Mullen, Director of health services for the New Mexico Department of Health and the Environment, described a world previously unknown to me. "Based on death records alone," he began, "six residents of the state died last year due to malnutrition. . . . That's just what we know about. It was probably far more than that."

A woman covering our visit for the city newspaper whispered to me, "Is six deaths a year a lot? I know any death is bad, but is six really a lot?" Later, I was able to take time to explain what we already had learned. "Doctors rarely list malnutrition as a contributing cause on death certificates and malnourished bodies succumb to other diseases. So while an underlying cause of death may be nutritional deficiency, the attending physician will list 'pneumonia' as the diagnosis. But if a person is malnourished, the immune system will not function normally, so when we hear there are six cases of nutrition-related death we know it's only the tip of the iceberg."

Fitzhugh Mullen's presentation was dispassionate, but his face betrayed the anger he felt. Formerly the Director of the National Health Service Corps, a program that places doctors in medically underserved communities, Mullen was aware of the adverse results of recent federal budget cuts. "In New Mexico, twenty-four percent of the infants and twenty-three percent of the older children on WIC are underweight. Thirty-six percent are below the fifth percentile for growth, a sign of chronic malnutrition. Nearly all the pregnant women are anemic, and many have to receive blood transfusions before they deliver." These facts mask an even more unsettling situation, since WIC children and mothers tend to be better off than the poor who are not on the program.

Buddy Gallegos, Director of the Roadrunner Food Bank and a short man with a strong will to help the needy, shifted gears to talk about the growing demand for emergency food among the poor. Wearing a bright shirt, the color of the Navajo ring on his hand, he said simply, "We don't have enough food to feed all the people in Albuquerque who need it. School counselors call me to say the children are anemic and hungry. They ask us to help the family with meals. We do our best, but it's not always enough."

As we were leaving, the reporter who had asked me about malnutrition-related death insisted I follow her outside and down a nearby hill. "It's not just the children who are hungry around here," she said, pointing to the space beneath a bridge. "I just wrote a story about this. Over forty people sleep down there every night. Some of them are families with kids."

Our next stop in Albuquerque was across town, to meet

with Dr. Carol Geil, Medical Director of the Young Children's Health Center. The city's clinics frequently distribute food because so many patients are hungry and undernourished, she told us. "We have mothers who can't even afford the Jell-O we prescribe for infant diarrhea."

She went on to say that the clinic staff had recently conducted a survey of families seeking medical services through the Health Center. "Our results confirmed what we'd been hearing from the emergency food programs. When we asked parents whether they ever went hungry so their children could eat, seventy-nine percent said yes. Most described living on limited, often uncertain incomes, and working very hard to find and use all available resources for the family. Most of them also said that food stamps, if they received them at all, ran out before the end of the month. . . . The mothers we interviewed said things like, 'My husband is a construction worker and he's not working steadily. I go hungry most of the time lately so the kids can eat.' Or, 'My husband is from Mexico so we don't get any benefits. Things are tight when he is out of work and we sometimes don't have any grocery money. One week we had only beans.' Another said, 'My welfare payment is only five dollars more than my rent. The food stamps just don't last.'"

As Dr. Geil spoke, I couldn't help thinking of the absurdity of doctors and medical staff having to hand out food in America. Yet we already had heard the same story in other places, and years ago I had seen the practice in India, while working in the Peace Corps. But that had been years ago, in faraway village clinics. This was America. Yet, we had seen Navajo children whose frail, brown bodies were like those of the children from halfway around the world.

"I WANT TO GO TO WORK, NOT THE MOON"

We began at six-thirty the next morning, standing in a line of approximately 150 people outside the Good Shepherd

Refuge in Albuquerque. Most, it seemed, were in their twenties and thirties, confirming Carol Geil's observations of the day before. The morning air was cool and dry, giving no warning of the intense heat that would follow as the sun rose higher. Waiting for the doors to open, we spent fifteen minutes mingling with those in line, learning about the day-to-day circumstances of their lives.

We entered and soon found ourselves sitting with guests at several long tables. Three priests watched; they seemed pleased at the spectacle of the out-of-state doctors sharing a meal of hot cereal, toast, and coffee with the hungry. The press recorded the entire event.

Across from me sat thirty-year-old Robert, a teacher now out of work. He declined to give me his last name, perhaps out of embarrassment about his predicament. "When teaching jobs were cut back in Salt Lake City," he said, "I came to Albuquerque. I had been told that there was work here. The reports were wrong. I've been trying to get a job teaching and there's nothing around."

"Maybe he should go into space?" teased the man sitting next to me, referring to President Reagan's recent announcement that the first civilian in space would be a teacher.

Robert looked into his oatmeal and managed a small chuckle. "Space?" he asked incredulously, "I don't want to go to the moon, I want to work."

"I live in an outside jail," another man chimed in spontaneously. "I got no money, no phone. I go to apply for jobs, but employers can't call me and I can't call them. Shopkeepers keep me away from their stores because they think I'll scare off the customers. I have a hard time finding a place to sleep. The city should start its own factory, just to hire people like me who want to work."

An interesting idea I thought, as I asked his line of work.

"I was a shop foreman for eleven years."

The Fathers at Good Shepherd said they had begun providing meals in 1981, serving about one hundred guests daily. By 1984, they were serving more than four hundred.

After the breakfast meeting, we drove off to visit other emergency feeding programs in the area. At the First Baptist Church, Mike McEuen said he recently had established a feeding program with the expectation of feeding about fifty guests, but more than three hundred showed up the first day. Each program confirmed the pattern we already had seen in so many other cities across the nation: the demand for emergency food was increasing at an alarming pace.

During the afternoon we began the first of our visits to local schools. At the Kit Carson Elementary School, the nurse told us that more and more children were coming to her complaining of stomach pain because they were hungry. "Their symptoms are easily relieved when I give them some food," she said.

We heard similar reports from teachers and nurses at the Harrison and Ernie Pyle middle schools. Staff member Vida Aceveda summed up the common experience by saying, "In Albuquerque, teachers now prepare sacks of food on Friday because the children don't get enough to eat at home over the weekend."

One of the nurses pulled Steve Berman aside to tell him about her families. "We randomly called fifty mothers to ask about the school lunch program. Many stated that during weekends their children get only one meal a day. Some cried while trying to explain they lacked the resources to feed their children on the weekends and during summer when school is not in session. For many of the children, school lunch is their one meal of the day."

A school nurse and two teachers commented on the effect of new federal regulations, which forced children off the school lunch program by requiring families to begin paying a small amount for school lunches. "When the cost of the school lunch was raised from twenty cents to forty cents," one of the teachers said, "a lot of children stopped eating because they could not afford the increase."

An elementary school principal gave an example. "Just today, two little boys came to see me after lunch to say they were still hungry. I looked down at their twenty-two-inch waists and told them to get back in line again." She seemed proud that she had defied federal regulations by letting the children get a second helping.

My group sat in on a number of classes to hear discussions about hunger and poverty. In Ms. Johnson's eighth grade honors class Rosie Gonzales blurted, "The government should do something to end hunger. It's not fair for Reagan to cut money from my family just because we're poor and he's rich." Chad, a talkative blond boy, added, "Our leaders are so worried about getting killed by the Russians that they're letting Americans die in a lot of other ways."

Our next stop was to meet with health professionals at the Albuquerque Family Health Center. Dr. Leman, the Medical Director, gathered us around a table to report that the lack of food is a serious problem among his patients and is especially severe among undocumented aliens. Public health nurse Teresa Lazarin added, "We see children hospitalized due to lack of food. Some mothers bring their babies straight from the maternity ward to us because there's no food in the house. Then, back they go to the hospital. . . . Some children make it," she continued, "but at the expense of the mother's health. Parents generally forego food for themselves in order to save it for the children. We recently saw a woman who basically starved herself to feed her child."

The clinic's nutritionist reported that 30 to 40 percent of their children are anemic. A staff physician added that some children are normal until age two. But thereafter, they fall off the normal range on the growth charts because they do not get enough to eat.

While we were visiting health clinics and schools, Naomi Kistin and another doctor were calling on Local 40 of the

Sheetmetal Workers. Unemployed worker Bob Voss told her, "I was laid off from my work at Kirkland Air Force Base fifteen months ago. My unemployment ran out and my wife had a nervous breakdown. We had no money coming in and my three kids were dependent on the school lunch program. We didn't qualify for welfare. . . . They make you have ZERO," he said vehemently, "before they give you any emergency help. That makes it harder to bounce back and more likely to perpetuate your being on welfare. I'd rather be a tax contributor than a tax taker. It makes you bitter the stuff they put you through to get any help."

"WHY MAKE IT SO DIFFICULT FOR THEM?"

Our last stop that night was at Casa Armijo, a community agency serving the poor in the South Valley area. One Casa worker's statement summed up what we had heard all day, "Our valley is a hungry valley." I spoke with parents who had come to request food for that evening. Some had already been denied food stamps, others felt intimidated because they were here illegally. "When we go for help," one woman reported, "it's because we need it, not because we want to. We get trouble but no food."

At an earlier public meeting, state Secretary of Human Services Juan Vigil brought up problems with the food stamp program. His frank statements echoed what we already had been hearing in other localities: woefully inadequate benefit levels and bureaucratic obstacles work together to prevent needy people from obtaining assistance. "The problem is not that people getting food stamps don't know how to handle their money. They've been doing it since they were married. The problem is they don't have enough. It just doesn't last any more.

"Poverty increased in New Mexico over the past few years," Vigil elaborated, "to over seventeen percent statewide and more than that in certain areas. Yet as poverty went up, the federal government made it harder for us to serve the poor. Rather than weeding out cheats the rules kept hungry people off the program."

Vigil added one especially tragic note, "In this area the land means so much to the culture of the people. Yet those poor people who own some land find it prevents them from getting public assistance. The government assesses the value of their land and says they are not eligible for assistance programs. The land, however, produces little real income. Usually it is used just for a little grazing. Mostly, its value is in the tradition of passing it on to future generations." As I heard these words I had images of the striking landscape we had seen upon our arrival. I could understand its importance as a cultural force, even though the desert vistas have little income potential.

"I don't understand," a local professional exclaimed at the meeting. "If we know there's so much poverty and hunger, why do we have to make it so difficult for them?"

"A BABY DIES AND NO ONE KNOWS"

We flew from Albuquerque to South Texas, with an exhausting seven-hour nighttime layover in Dallas. Our center for operations in south Texas was the border town of Harlingen, a heavily Chicano city of approximately 35,000 near the Rio Grande River. There we would be joined by local physicians who would serve as guides and colleagues during our stay. Immediately after arrival we dispatched one team to El Paso, in West Texas; we planned to rendezvous later in Houston.

Harlingen lies in a fertile valley approximately 70 miles long by 30 miles wide at the southernmost tip of the state. The winters are mild and summers hot, conditions that produce large harvests of fruit and vegetables that are sold in supermarkets throughout the United States. Mechanization in the agricultural industry, however, has led to substantial unemployment, swelling the pool of migrant laborers who head north a few months each year to seek work. Local officials estimate that up to 40 percent of the workers remain out of work during the winter months.

The sun bore down as we made our rounds in town. The almost overwhelming bright light seemed to illuminate the hidden despair of the residents. José Rodriguez, one of the local doctors, explained, "Hunger in the Southwest is usually not blatant. It is not visible to the public eye as a pot-bellied starving person, but rather as a discreet epidemic which is spreading."

We stopped at Su Clínica ("Your Clinic"), which serves many Chicano residents. Rampant poverty and unemployment was evident in the waiting list of eight hundred families needing the low-cost care provided by the clinic. For the most part, no one working in Texas agriculture receives health care benefits; few make even the minimum wage. A representative of the Archdiocese explained that most farmworkers get less than a dollar fifty an hour for working long days in pesticide-infested fields. "Many of the growers pay by check," he said, "but show fewer hours put in than the people actually work. It looks as though they are paying federal minimum wage." Under these conditions it is not surprising that the workers' families cannot afford to pay for health care.

"Life in the area," we heard from Stanley Fisch, a transplanted northern doctor, "is marginal at best. The infant mortality rate is listed as somewhat better than the overall Texas average, but the figure is wrong. Many, if not most, of the deaths are not counted. A baby dies and is buried, but no one outside the family ever knows."

Clinic dietician Gwen Olson elaborated, "I've worked in many Third World nations, including Egypt and Colombia. There are many parallels between what I saw in those areas and what we see here. A lot of children experience growth failure because they don't get enough to eat. It is just like South America."

In the face of this poverty, even small efforts to tip the tenuous balance between life and death often make a great difference, Fisch explained. "WIC supplemental feeding is one of those programs. When the children are getting WIC benefits they improve dramatically; when they don't, their small bodies display it visibly."

We left Su Clínica with our local guides for the *"colonias,"* unincorporated communities housing the poorest in the Harlingen area. The majority of residents are young families, a good number of them undocumented immigrants. The homes are cheap structures that lack running water and sewage services. The fortunate families have a small plot of land on which to plant a garden. Bill Beardslee noted that the *colonias* seem a wild parody of the American Dream, mocking the wealthy suburbs where each family has land and a home.

Our first stop was at the home of Mrs. Chavez, mother of eight school-age children, all of whom were in school when we arrived. Mr. Chavez is disabled, the victim of an accident that damaged his hearing and sight. He sat quietly in the other room as Mrs. Chavez explained through an interpreter that he had been denied disability insurance because the state decided he is only 70 percent disabled. The Chavez family was left trying to make it on $500 a month, largely from food stamps. Of this amount, $35 went each month for rent; their house, a three-room shack whose only source of water was a dripping outdoor spigot approximately 30 feet away, partially concealed by a thicket of weeds.

Mrs. Chavez continued sporadically to do the laundry as we conversed. The press recorded our visit. I looked around, noting a pile of clothing and shoes that had been delivered by a church group. Using my halting Spanish, I learned that the family had eaten only rice and beans for breakfast. Some days the children get milk, but they had had no fresh fruit or vegetables for a week and a half.

When asked about the children's health, the mother paused before confessing that her eleven-year-old son's broken arm had never been set. When they went to a nearby health clinic for treatment, they had been turned away because they did not have the $9 fee. The local hospital refused to care for the child because the family could not produce a $250 deposit. "His arm is healing," she said, "but it does not look good."

As we listened, a local shop owner who knew of the family's circumstances leaned over and said to me, "How is it possible to have these problems in America?" I wondered if she knew that more than thirty-five million Americans lack health-care insurance. The Chavez family's situation was hardly unique.

Something about Mrs. Chavez made me tarry as my team members and the reporters departed. I asked to see where she prepares her meals, and she led me to a back room with a dirt floor, a refrigerator, and a wooden table. I gestured for permission to open the refrigerator and look inside. I found three tortillas, a container of water, and a cup of milk.

I asked what they would have for dinner that night. Mrs. Chavez pointed to the refrigerator. I reached into my pocket to hand her a twenty-dollar bill and thanked her for talking with us. Silently, she took it in hand. Her eyes smiled, but her lips barely parted as she murmured, "*Gracias.*" I had not done much. It would be another ten days before the family received more food stamps.

We then walked down the road a short distance and stopped at the home of seventy-eight-year-old Mr. Alviso, living with his wife and five-year-old granddaughter. Mr. Alviso said they once had received food stamps, but had been terminated from the program. He did not know why they had been deemed ineligible; judging from their living circumstances, it seemed unlikely the reason could have been their income. Each day the elderly man set out to collect bottles for redemption at a local store. With that money he bought food for the family.

"Do you have milk for your little girl?" I asked.

"No, *señor*," he answered.

"Do you buy milk for your family?" I followed.

"*Nunca, señor*," he replied. Never.

Their diet was rice, beans, and potatoes. Neither Mr. Alviso nor his wife could remember when they last had fresh vegetables. As Mr. Alviso described collecting bottles to buy food for his family, I thought of his similarity to Danny Holley. Except, of course, the old man was still alive.

We walked to the home of Mrs. Gonzales and her three children. Her husband was unemployed. The family was ineligible for public assistance and was surviving on food stamps. Mrs. Gonzales' brother and sister-in-law helped with their $35 monthly rent. Their street, like the others in the area, was unpaved.

"My children look forward to school," she said, "because they receive lunch and breakfast. During the summer and weekends there is only enough food in the house to give them one meal a day. I can give them only rice, beans, tortillas, or noodles." Steve looked into her refrigerator to find a half-empty bag of tortillas, some cheese, a small amount of milk and butter. In the kitchen was lard and a bit of spaghetti. The food we saw would have to last them a week, until they received another food stamp allotment.

An hour later we sat in the living room of Urbano Cortez and his wife. At age sixty-seven, Mr. Cortez provided for his wife, daughter, and granddaughter on $367 in social security and $125 in food stamps. As we chatted he characterized his circumstances as "so wonderful, three times better than when I was younger." As Steve conversed with the man I wondered what groceries they could afford on so little income.

"What will you eat today?" Steve queried.

"Rice, beans, and potatoes. Every day," he replied, smiling.

"Three times a day?" Steve questioned.

"My doctor said I should eat fresh fruit, but we can't afford it. If we did have the money, I'd buy the fruit and give it to my granddaughter. . . . I started working when I was six years old and didn't stop until I was sixty-two," he said. "I started out as a water carrier and ended up a supervisor earning sixty dollars a week. I worked for a packing company until the plant closed down. When they went out of business I got no pension for fifty-six years of service. But, I can still work, if I can find a job. I've been hearing since I was five years old that Mexican-Americans don't want to work," Mr. Cortez continued. "But whenever jobs are available they are always filled, even if people have to travel north to get them." As we left his house, we remarked on the irony that a man who worked from age six to sixty-two felt he had to defend his willingness to work.

Shortly after our visit, Mr. Cortez died. We learned that it had not been a dramatic death and could be attributed to no single cause. Although Mr. Cortez had often known hunger, he certainly had not starved to death or died from outright malnutrition. The tragedy in my mind was that for him, and so many others, working a lifetime does not guarantee security or even a minimal livelihood in old age.

News of his premature death gave a special note of sadness to our Texas field investigation.

"They Become Human Garbage Here"

Our next stop was in the border city of Brownsville, where we met with local health and social service professionals at the office of the Archdiocese. "Hunger in our valley is widespread," reported a priest. "It is worse than any time in the last fifteen years."

"The infrastructure for helping the poor is very weak here," another church worker said. "Federal efforts always have fallen short, but recent cutbacks have aggravated the situation. The worst problems are with the food stamp program."

"People have to apply in person," explained the social services director of a local agency. "Then they are told to return in ten days. If they are five minutes late, which is easy since most don't have a car, their appointment is canceled. If they are denied food stamps and appeal, they have to wait two or three months before they even get a hearing. During

the interim period the family usually has little to eat, sometimes just about nothing." The director paused, frowned, and
expressed his frustration. "It seems like things are set up to
keep people from getting help."

Alicia Montez, a social service worker at the LaJolla Elderly Center, described their efforts at emergency feeding.
"Because it is so difficult to get food stamps, we feel the
pressure on our agency. People begin lining up the night
before we serve food. But we can serve only fifty people, so
many get turned away. Yet, they still come. . . . Mr. Meese
says that people come to soup kitchens just because the food
is free," she added. "He might change his mind if he came
to our center and saw elderly people waiting in line all night
to get a meal."

Sitting at the outer edge of the circle of chairs the principal
of a local elementary school spoke next. "I was a teacher for
eighteen years before I became school principal, and I've lived
in this community for more than a decade. Today, most of
the kids come to school hungry. It is worse now than at any
time since I've been here. Ninety-five percent of the time it
is because the parents can't afford to buy enough food. . . .
Hunger exists because no one seems to think it is important,"
he went on. In his analysis, "No one wants to try to take silent,
subservient people and help to turn them around. If they get
over being hungry they may want other things. It's easier to
keep them like they are."

The principal stopped speaking to let an Indian-born physician from a local health center speak. "The poor people here
become human garbage. They are damned. The majority of
our patients wander all over America as migrant workers. They
pick crops, but can't afford to buy the fruits and vegetables
they harvest. They breathe pesticides while they work, but
no one cares. They sleep without beds and have no toilets
and no medical care. Their children get no education."

One in five of his patients has chronic ear problems that
can lead to deafness. Many have roundworms, pinworms, or

infectious hepatitis. About 25 percent are anemic; 80 percent never get dental care. After reciting these figures from prepared notes he concluded with an anecdote from his homeland. "I'm told that elephants don't die of disease; they die of starvation when their teeth fall out. That also happens to some of my patients." His startling analogy left a hush in the room.

I pondered my earlier conversation with him. When he learned I had worked in India while in the Peace Corps, we enjoyed a few minutes' conversation in Hindi, talking about life in the rural villages of his homeland. Now, I saw the irony of his telling about the tragic lives of impoverished Americans.

A nurse midwife from Raymondville broke the silence. "We've been seeing more and more pregnant women with anemia. Iron-rich foods such as raisins, apricots, and spinach are all priced too high for people to buy. It is impossible for our patients to eat correctly on the money they have. It has nothing to do with patient education; they just can't afford the food.

"We see a lot of obesity during pregnancy, but also some women who lose weight," she went on. "The obesity occurs because the women can afford only cheap, starchy food. It fills them up but doesn't provide adequate nutrition." The women that lose weight are the ones whose food stamps run out before the end of the month.

She testified that she had recently had a patient who dropped five pounds in two weeks, although she had warned the woman about losing weight during pregnancy. "The growing baby will rob your body of nutrients unless you eat properly," she had said. "But sister," the patient told her, "I'm already watering down the milk for my other children. I can't drink it myself."

"THEY CHOOSE BETWEEN FOOD AND WATER"

Meanwhile, across the state, Bill, Aaron, and José were conducting their work in the border city of El Paso and finding it impossible to separate hunger from other factors related to poverty. In a *colonia* just outside the city, blue-collar people were deprived of running water in their homes and forced to drink from containers atop large delivery trucks. Marked "toxic substance" because of the agricultural pesticides they had once held, the containers now were being used for water storage. "A lot of the people here have to choose between food and water," a minister explained. "Often there isn't money for both."

On the first morning, the doctors met at a community agency. Amy Costillo from the Council on Aging told them, "In 1982 we began a program to distribute free cheese. It came in ten-pound boxes. We were so overwhelmed with requests we had to divide the packages into thirds. But, even with these efforts, we estimate that ten thousand elderly people in El Paso who are eligible for some form of public assistance don't get any help whatsoever. Many are afraid to apply, because they are undocumented immigrants. They may have been here for thirty years but they still don't have papers."

A nun from a local parish elaborated on the problems of undocumented immigrants. "When people can find work their wages are very low, but they can't apply for food stamps. So, they're hungry. Through our food bank we distribute $250,000 in food a year and our church gives out $33,000 in emergency cash assistance. But, that's still not enough. . . . When the farmworkers strike to make their lives better, their children go hungry," she added. "When they're not in school they scrounge around the supermarkets and dumpsters looking for food."

As they moved on to make home visits, José met with Mrs. Gonzales, who lived alone with her three children. Conversing with her in Spanish, he learned that she and the two oldest children are undocumented aliens. "I have tried many times to work as a maid for rich people who live on the other side of town. But, I am always harassed by the Border Patrol. Many times I have to hide, so I miss the bus that takes me to work. I applied for food stamps, but get them only for my youngest, who is a citizen. Sometimes this little bit is all I have for the four of us for the month. I just want the freedom to work to support my family. Most people with legal status or who are U.S. citizens don't want to work as a maid. Why can't I? I won't be hurting anyone."

After speaking with Mrs. Gonzales, José recounted his experience providing medical care in the community. "On the surface the people may appear to be well nourished. They are obese. But they often have high levels of triglycerides and cholesterol. Their diet consists of refried beans, tortillas, rice, and potatoes. They eat what they can and stretch it as much as possible. As many as thirty percent of the children in this part of town are anemic."

The group stopped by a tiny office on a side street to speak with striking farmworkers. About twenty members of the union had come, describing with dignity and anger the exploitation of farmworker life. In order to toil in the fields, the workers must be on the street by midnight, assembling in a small area of a few blocks near the El Paso bridge. The bosses drive up in buses and pick out who they want to work for them. The process may go on for three hours before the bus is full. The selection process is arbitrary. The work is painful, and there is no minimum wage. The workers are paid for what they pick. Six containers of green chilies yield the worker a red chip; at the end of the day, the chips are counted and paid off in cash. The pay is well below minimum wage and when transport time is counted, it is even lower. Some of the bosses will not bring drinkable water into the field, but instead sell beer at high prices to the workers.

"The workers," Bill Beardslee later explained, "have no control over the way they are treated. There is no consistency, either. Because the workers are paid in cash they never have any check or written documentation of their wages. That means difficulties if they need to apply for unemployment or food stamps.

"I want to emphasize," Bill stressed, "the dignity of the workers we met, but also the edge of anger in their voices. At the end we came back to the subject of hunger, which they knew had prompted our visit. One of the workers said, 'People talk about a balanced diet, but there is nothing to balance in our diet.' "

A short time after my colleagues left El Paso, the head of the city's medical society wrote a letter to Harvard to complain about our fieldwork. He felt reports in the local newspaper had exaggerated the severity of conditions in the area. I read over his letter several times before replying. I asked him to provide us with whatever data he had on the nutritional status of people in the community. His failure to respond reminded me of the physician in Greenwood, Mississippi, who had said there was no hunger in the area. All the blacks he knew were "fat and shiny."

"A MILLION HUNGRY TEXANS"

The next day our group reunited in Houston for a final round of fieldwork. For me it was a homecoming of sorts, because I had lived there for six years of my childhood. As we traveled in the greater Houston area I found the glitter and growth that had occurred in the interim astonishing. Much of the sparkle was to prove misleading, however. A recent and precipitous drop in oil prices, slowdowns in the space program, and unemployment in traditional industries had combined to replace the booming 1970s with economic stagnation and hard times in the 1980s. We had come to Houston because it is an international symbol of American affluence in a state with many wealthy and middle-class families. The contrasts between rich and poor, therefore, stand out more dramatically than in the relatively poorer states of the Mississippi Delta and Appalachia. During the expansion years, unemployed workers from "rust belt" states had flocked to the area seeking economic opportunity, an influx reminiscent of the migration of people from Oklahoma to California in the Great Depression.

By the time of our visit, the good times were decidedly over. Those who had been poor remained that way; many previously middle-class families now found themselves in the uncomfortable position of joining the ranks of the "new poor" and learning firsthand the anti-welfare bias of state government. The stinginess and adversarial attitudes of the public assistance programs reminded us of our experiences in North Carolina.

Our first stop in Houston was at a public hearing opened by State Senator Hugh Parmer, whose Select Hunger Committee had recently released a report describing the desperate straits for poor Texans. "These aren't Harvard graduates," the Senator described the poor. "I'm absolutely convinced we're using red tape to turn away literally thousands of people who are in dire need of emergency food."

Their bipartisan study, documenting an escalating epidemic of hunger across the state, estimated that the demand for emergency food had gone up 300 percent from 1980 to 1984. In some areas the need had increased far more. The number of "new poor" had reached previously unheard of numbers. Yet the state was doing little to help. Of the 814,000 women and children eligible for WIC, for instance, only about 20 percent were being served.

"Seven of the ten leading causes of death in Texas are believed to be linked to nutritional status," Parmer pointed out. "The Texas Department of Health recently documented over five hundred deaths, primarily among elderly persons, due to malnutrition over the prior three years. From what we know about death certificates this means that many more people are silently suffering from malnutrition."

Our briefing ended with some sobering statistics that reflected the state's attitude toward the poor. Only one-fourth of Texas's two million people living in poverty obtain *any* form of public assistance. Almost one million people in the state, the majority of them children, regularly go hungry.

"We're the New Poor and We're Pissed off"

Outside the Armco Steel plant we found a huge billboard proclaiming: "HOUSTON WORKS." Inside the union hall sat a group of burly steelworkers who were unemployed. "More than five thousand people lost their jobs when the plant closed," a union official said. "Mostly, they are men and women who had worked for the company for decades. These workers used to be middle-class and now they're losing everything." Most of the former workers had exhausted their unemployment benefits.

"We're running out of options," reported Bart, a strapping man of about thirty-five. "For some of us the next stop is the middle of the river." When he had work, Bart earned $30,000 a year; he and his wife and five children lived well on that income. For the past two years he had been without income, the family living on rice and cornmeal. "I may not look hungry," he said, acknowledging that he had gained fifty pounds on the inadequate diet. "But I am, all the time."

Thirty-six-year-old Dave Edwards spoke up. "One of my kids is a diabetic; he needs insulin. I've been out of work for two years and my health insurance has run out. It's been near impossible to feed the family, much less buy insulin."

"We want jobs, not welfare," a worker yelled across the room to no one in particular.

Ella Person chimed in, "I've worked in this industry for twenty-three years and never asked anyone for help. My husband was injured on the job, and he's out of work, too." She reached into her pocket and held out her hand to show three pennies. "This is literally all we've got," she said. "Three cents and two hungry kids."

"It seems that you are angry," one of my colleagues ventured. "In other places we've visited people seemed more shy, you know, reluctant to say what's on their minds."

"Yeah," responded Joe Anderson, "We're the new poor and we're pissed off. We've got a lot of pride and don't like what is happening. Some fathers have had to fake leaving their children so the family could get welfare. How do you think it feels to have to commit fraud to get a little help? We've worked a lot of years—too many to be treated like this."

The anger was understandable, but it was not the only emotion with which they wrestled. They also were depressed, quite despondent. "Sometimes," one man said, "I wish I could just go to sleep and never wake up."

"THE HUNGRY LOOK LIKE US"

We traveled on toward suburban Pasadena to visit a food pantry where the Salvation Army serves a thousand families each week. The director said that many of the families are formerly middle-class. "One man drove up in a Lincoln Continental and asked for food. My staff asked why I gave him a bag of groceries. That car was all he had. He had lost his job, then his home, and finally his wife. He was living in the car and he was hungry."

Unaccustomed to unemployment, hunger, and poverty, the newly poor feel cast out by society. Reverend Steve Cartwright, who runs a church food pantry, spoke about his community. "When we first started up three years ago, we found the hungry were not those we anticipated. The hungry look like us. They drive cars and they dress well. You can imagine what it's like for them to be hungry and have no money."

Just as Cartwright predicted, when we drove around the tree-lined streets of Pasadena it was almost impossible to believe that hunger could exist in the town. The lawns and hedges were neatly trimmed, the house appeared well kept. The community bore no obvious imprint of poverty. It was another thing to go inside the houses.

We met Mrs. Guerra, whose unemployed husband took whatever carpentry jobs he could find. "Once the food stamps run out," she reported, "we stop eating fruit, and there are no snacks for the children. We can spend an entire week eating a little chicken and a lot of potatoes. Our doctor said my two-year-old is anemic, but let me tell you," she pointed her finger to the outside, "a lot of people are worse off than us."

"What would help?" I asked.

"A job for my husband. But, if not that, at least make the system more humane."

"What do you mean?" Bill Beardslee chimed in.

"The food stamp system makes things too hard. You go through the application process and then get told 'no.' You appeal and go through it again and finally they give you some food stamps. But, it's not really enough. One month we were cut off because my husband got a little work. He reported his wages, but was paid in cash so he couldn't prove the amount. He could have lied. We were penalized because he was honest. What's the point?"

Our next stop was to the home of the Boyds, a young white couple that had come to Houston from Mississippi in search of work. We sat and chatted in their carpeted living room, while their three boys, ages five, six, and nine, listened. "We eat beans, rice, and gravy, but no fruit and few vegetables," Mrs. Boyd said. "We're not deprived of food, but I know the children aren't eating properly. I just can't buy *good* food."

"I work full-time at minimum wage," Mr. Boyd added.

"We rely on food stamps. We couldn't make it without them." The longer we spoke, the more Mr. Boyd seemed to withdraw. When I asked what it felt like to be unable to buy enough food for his sons, he stared hard at the carpet and lost his composure.

Traveling with us was Steve Glauber, the executive producer of *60 Minutes*, a nice man, but also a tough New Yorker. He was trying to determine whether *60 Minutes* should do a story on national hunger. As Mr. Boyd began to cry I could feel everyone in the room tense. The television producer made a cutting gesture with his open hand, commanding the cameraman to turn off the lights; it was a compassionate act for someone whose job it is to capture just such moments on film. The room was quiet until I broke the silence to thank the family for letting us come into their home.

As we filed out, Bill stopped me in the driveway and said we should return to talk with the family in private. Inside the living room Bill spoke softly to Mr. Boyd. "You're obviously doing everything you can to care for your family. Sometimes you may feel like you're a failure, even when you try as hard as you can. But, sometimes things happen for awhile that are just out of your control. Remember that hard times are not your fault. You're a good father."

After listening quietly, Mr. Boyd thanked us for coming back. Bill and I felt a little better, but for hours we remained saddened and disquieted. In a way, our hectic schedule was a blessing; there just was not enough time to become overwhelmed by our emotions.

Back in Houston later that evening, our guide reported seeing many families like the Boyds. "We run an emergency food pantry and see that all the time. People come in, and when you open them up a little they break down and cry. Giving food to people sends a message, whether you mean it or not. It says they cannot feed their families. That message really hurts."

During the day we had become impressed with the efforts

of local agencies valiantly trying to deal with the problems of hunger, homelessness, and poverty. But we also learned that the response of some could be difficult to comprehend. The Houston Light and Power Company, for instance, began giving customers who could not pay their bills the names and phone numbers of churches providing assistance to the poor, instructing these customers to ask already strained programs for help in paying the utility bills.

"They tried to make us their collection agency," a priest protested. "The Company, along with other utilities in the area, developed a 'Share Program.' For every dollar contributed by the public, the utilities would donate a dollar. But the utilities used the money to pay themselves, not to purchase food and services needed by the poor. On top of that, they took a tax write-off for their portion of the contribution."

"It's just obscene," one of the priest's co-workers added. "They had no shame about what they were doing."

We also learned that just before our visit an error by the state's computer had denied food stamps to approximately three thousand eligible families. Instead of providing a quick correction, state officials suggested that recipients appeal to church pantries for assistance. The small agencies were overwhelmed by the people the state's error had hurt.

A woman from Conroe, Texas, spoke about the problems of the undocumented immigrants, many of them from war-torn Central America, who do not receive government-sponsored food benefits. Because they are afraid of being deported, the illegal aliens seldom ask anyone for help and never apply to government agencies. And the churches that assist the undocumented aliens face possible federal prosecution.

"The government lets them into the country," she said, "but prosecutes its own citizens who respond to their human tragedy." Several months after our field visit, the Justice Department indicted a number of priests, nuns, and lay workers who had been providing help and sanctuary to Central American refugees.

"WE NEED SELFLESS LEADERS"

Our final field visit in Houston was with members of the city health department. The meeting had been scheduled at a church because a number of department employees had been concerned that a public discussion of the health consequences of hunger would produce negative publicity. Despite warnings from certain city officials, a large number of professionals showed up and openly discussed their experiences.

Mrs. d'Feranti, head of the city's nutrition programs, told us that "The ill health we see in the city is often directly related to hunger. The federal government cut back on the number of pregnant women and infants who could be enrolled in the WIC feeding program from ten thousand to just over seven thousand. In my mind it is an unavoidable conclusion that this has contributed to the increased number of babies born below normal weight and is related to higher infant mortality."

Just prior to our visit the infant mortality rate had increased for the first time in years. Among the poor, the number of infant deaths was considerably higher than in the rest of the city. At the Riverside Health Center, which serves a low-income community, for instance, the infant mortality rate was more than double the national average and higher than in some Third World countries. The disparity in infant deaths between rich and poor is often a ghastly manifestation of an epidemic of hunger.

"We also are seeing the results of hunger and malnutrition in our clinics," said health worker Barbara Jacobs. She told us about a Department study conducted prior to our arrival, which found that over half the infants in one poor neighborhood were anemic. In another low-income community it was discovered that among the children one to five years of age, 70 percent were drinking too little milk and 90 percent were getting inadequate amounts of fruits and vegetables.

Just before leaving the state we met with reporters and community representatives in the church basement that houses the Texas Anti-Hunger Coalition. The chairs were filled, and a number of people stood around the edges of the hall. The press conference proved to be cathartic, helping us focus our thoughts and relieve pent-up emotions. Before taking questions from the audience I introduced our group and made several remarks. "Texas," I pointed out, "ranks near the bottom of the states on the amount it spends per person on medical care and public assistance for the poor. Federal cutbacks have hurt, but they have affected other states, too. My impression is that Texas—although certainly not all of its people—is a wealthy state with a stingy heart."

Aaron spoke next, comparing his observations on this trip with experiences from a Task Force investigation in 1967. "What disturbs me most is that we see more people in jeopardy now, more living just on the brink. There seems to be less hope, too."

As a psychiatrist, Bill quickly picked up on Aaron's insight. "What worries me is that so many families seem to have no vision of the future. Nothing sustains them and their children. When we lose a vision of the future we lose the capacity to function well in the present." We had seen many Texans who were living on the edge. The unemployed steelworkers. The Boyd family. The angry farmworkers. Many seemed to have lost hope that things would someday be better.

Houston's rush-hour traffic was backed up along the route to the airport, and those of us heading back to Boston missed our flight. The 90-minute delay meant that I would not arrive in time to see my two children before they went to sleep. I was very disappointed. I missed them and was worried that I had been spending too much time away from home. I felt a bit better when one of my colleagues reminded me of the many hungry children we had met who rarely have happy reunions with their parents—children like Danny Holley, whose daily lives are immeasurably tarnished by poverty.

Just before falling asleep on the flight my last thought was of Mr. Cortez, the old man who would die a few weeks later. I had asked him what he thought should be done to make things better for himself and his grandchildren.

"What recommendations do you have for the nation?" I asked.

The old man who had been working full-time from early childhood pondered a moment before responding. "I would say that what we need most are jobs and transportation. We should start locally and then nationally. But, most of all, what we need are selfless leaders who see the suffering and do something about it."

5

Empty Plates in the Breadbasket

HERE IS a special irony in the presence of hunger in the breadbasket of our nation. The bountiful crops spring so abundantly from the fertile land that millions of tons of grain are stored at government expense, and the farms of the heartland produce millions of pounds of surplus dairy products even as the federal government institutes a program in which dairy farmers must slaughter their cows to curtail excess production. Yet within the very shadow of this vast productive system Americans, some the families who once worked the land, go hungry.

Illinois and Missouri were the final stops on our initial fourteen-state itinerary. While we were impatient to be finished with the work we had begun nearly two years before, we knew it was essential to see the face of hunger in the Midwest. For most of us it was almost inconceivable that there could be hunger in America's model rural hamlets and towns, places synonymous with wholesome values and secure, middle-class living. The complexities of hunger in the heartland would bring us back to South Dakota and Iowa the following year to study the food stamp program and see for ourselves the crisis separating farm families from their land.

"A Battlefield Report"

We began our work at Chicago's Cook County Hospital, a huge, sprawling complex of buildings located downtown in the nation's third largest city. We were warmly welcomed by Chief of Medicine Dr. Stephen Nightingale, who began by recalling a newspaper article in which Chicagoans were described as being "quiched out" from too many lavish dinners at chic restaurants and dinner parties. "Here," Nightingale said, "we admit several hundred patients each year due to inadequate nutrition. At this hospital the patients don't pick at their food."

Brenda Chandler, a pediatric social worker in her late twenties, picked up on Nightingale's train of thought: "Patients and families come here reticent to say they are hungry. But once they feel able to open up to the staff they ask the social worker if they might have some food to eat."

"It's worse than that," said dietician Mary Jo Davis. "We have people come just to ask where the hospital leaves the garbage. We perform dietary recalls on our patients, asking them what they ate over the last three or four days. Many times the pages are completely blank."

"How frequently is hunger seen among the patient population?" Gordon Harper asked.

Reading through a stack of patient charts piled on a metal table, a hospital physician answered the question. "Here's a mother and three children who stuffed food into their mouths. They had had nothing to eat for three days."

Opening up the next file, he said, "This four-year-old is stunted in growth, has anemia and hair loss."

Picking up another chart at random, he read, "This one, a twenty-month-old infant, is failing to thrive; has one meal a day, usually soup."

Leafing through the worn pages of a fourth chart the doctor continued with little outward expression, "Pregnant woman, gained one pound over seven months."

We listened intently as he summarized more cases. "Mother of four; let's see, according to the admitting physician's notes, she decides each day on which two of the kids gets something to eat. This next one is a case of mine, a mother who is diluting the milk she gives to the babies. I told her not to water it down. She said, 'Doctor, I have to survive, my baby has to have something to eat.' "

Agnes Lattimer, Chief of Pediatrics at Cook County, who had accompanied us on our fieldwork in Tennessee and North Carolina, added, "We've had a twenty-three percent increase in the number of children admitted for failure-to-thrive over the last year." Another pediatrician interjected, "A third of the children we see in the emergency room are underweight or stunted in growth, and many of the infants have severe diarrhea and dehydration."

Dr. Jorge Prieto, who has practiced medicine in Chicago for more than two decades, emphasized, "Things are getting worse, not better. Last year there was a thirty-two percent increase in pulmonary tuberculosis. Nutrition in these cases is a chief causal factor. The TB that reappears after treatment is virtually by definition due to factors related to nutrition and poverty. . . . The hospital sometimes has twenty TB patients on the wards at one time. That was unheard of just a few years ago," Prieto said.

"They say we don't see kwashiorkor and marasmus in this country," announced Katherine Christoffel, Chairman of the Committee on Nutrition of the Illinois Chapter of the American Academy of Pediatrics, "but we do. I see fifteen or twenty cases a year in my hospital. We used to think these diseases were only seen in Third World countries."

"We also see kwashiorkor and marasmus [life-threatening diseases caused by malnutrition]," reported Howard Levy, Chief of Pediatrics at Mount Sinai Hospital. "I haven't seen those problems since I was overseas. The frequency of malnutrition is clearly on the rise in the last few years. We see more low-birth-weight babies and growth failure among children. And so much TB that my house staff is no longer excited by it. It upsets me that they are not excited and disturbed by this trend." Levy paused for a moment to reflect. "What we see are clear, measurable health effects of hunger and malnutrition, proof that more and more families do not have enough money to buy food."

Dr. Effie Ellis, a warm and genial black pediatrician with white hair, added strong words. "The problems I see are of serious proportions. The social service agencies are having to provide medicines and the hospitals have to give out food." No one missed the irony in the reversal of these customary professional roles.

As we filed out of the briefing session one of my colleagues whispered, "I felt like we were getting a firsthand battlefield report." I nodded, thinking to myself that while the people who worked at Cook County Hospital are wonderful, it would be a pleasure to leave. It had been a shocking introduction to the Midwest.

"Isn't This Genocide?"

Upon leaving the hospital we divided into four teams traveling by car with local guides to various community agencies. My group went first to Uptown Ministries, a church-sponsored social service organization in a working-class residential neighborhood. We squeezed past several families waiting in the foyer on our way to a dining room, where still other people were waiting to be seen. I introduced myself to the smiling nun who runs the program while my colleagues made their way to chat with waiting guests: a few elderly individuals, many young parents with children, a couple of teenagers. Her cheerful countenance changing, the sister assured me that "Hunger has increased dramatically this year."

Without hesitation, an eighty-one-year-old white woman who had been eavesdropping interrupted: "I come here because I need food for my husband. His doctor put him on a diet of bland foods that we can't afford on our income. We eat mostly grits and oatmeal. Once in awhile we get to eat beans and rice, but those foods aren't on his diet." Next to her sat a thirty-year-old white woman who nodded in accord as she stared at the floor. "I go without food so my three children can eat. They still go hungry sometimes."

The middle-aged black woman sitting next to her spoke openly about her distress. "I get only two hundred and ten dollars a month now. I used to earn twenty thousand a year from the post office, but then I got sick and had to have surgery. I never got well enough to get back to work. For twenty years I paid taxes to help other people and now I get almost nothing for it. I've been living like this for five years."

I prodded a twenty-year-old man who had come with his girlfriend and baby to share their circumstances. Uneasy and hesitant he said, "I quit school when I was fourteen to help my mother raise my brothers and sisters. Last month I made about three hundred dollars in odd jobs. It's not enough to pay rent and eat. We have no money left. We're hungry."

Ruddy-faced Mrs. Maloney, actually of American Indian heritage despite her Irish surname, added spontaneously, "I live in a one-bedroom apartment with my two children. My oldest daughter lives with us, too, and she has two children. We never have enough food, especially at the end of the month when our food stamps run out."

"The meals we eat are never more than beans, rice, macaroni and cheese," Mrs. Maloney continued, her body corroborating the starchy diet. "Two of the babies were anemic until we got on WIC. But when they got better they were taken off the program. It wasn't more than a few weeks before the doctor said they were anemic again."

Her six-month-old granddaughter had a rash that her doctor attributed to a vitamin deficiency. Naomi Kistin examined the rash and whispered to me that the baby could not hold its head steady, a sign of developmental retardation.

From Uptown Ministries, it was a drive of several blocks to the Traveler's Aid Office, where we talked with a young social worker. "My clients are mostly undocumented people who live in fear of being recognized and deported," said Hector Lopez. "Their lives are all negatives. They can't even get into the cheese lines, for fear of being shipped out of the country. They get no help of any kind."

Lopez pressed his point, "The INS [Immigration and Naturalization Service] says your children can stay, but *you* can't. In other words, they say the government will help your children, but only if you leave here and never see them again. These children are U.S. citizens, with rights guaranteed by the Constitution. What rights do they have without their parents?"

On down the street some thirty-five people were waiting for a hot meal in the basement of the Uptown Baptist Church, a soup kitchen. After a short greeting, the minister placed us behind a long table and asked that we serve the meal of goulash, noodles, and vegetables. After ladling out the food, we filled our own plates and sat with the guests at three long picnic-style tables.

I sat next to Sterling Banks, who held his head about six inches from the white plate while he shoveled in the food until it was gone. His cup of juice disappeared next, and then he wiped his mouth with a paper napkin. Having finished his meal, he looked up into my face and said, "I won't let my children eat here. I got no job, but I still have my pride. I don't eat any food at home so they can eat what we have. Thank God I can get one meal a day here." As we talked, I learned that sometimes he did have to bring his children to the church soup kitchen. "I've brought them here the times we've had no food in the house."

He contemplated his own statement before adding, "No food. Mister, I mean NO food."

I caught the eye of an elderly man across from me. Through his T-shirt I could see none of the excess fat common to people his age. Almost apologetically he told how he appreciates the food but hates to come to get it. It hurt his pride. Edwin Meese's quip about "freeloaders" in soup kitchens came to mind as I looked at this grandfatherly figure, and I felt my anger rise. He and the other guests around me already felt like social outcasts. Why, I pondered, would a powerful official try to rob them of their final vestiges of self-esteem? Why the bullying of those who cannot answer back?

"The problem is disconnection," I overheard a young nun explaining to my colleague, Reverend Craig Biddle. "Those who can do something about hunger in this country are disconnected from those who can't help themselves." Craig said he appreciated her feelings, but rejected her metaphysical analysis of the hunger epidemic. "The Mayor's Office," Craig said, "says there are up to eight hundred thousand hungry people in this city. A problem of this magnitude can't really be summarized as disconnection."

Later, the director of a national food bank network headquartered in Chicago gave a more concrete appraisal. "It's an American tragedy. When we see government agencies cutting back their programs and referring people to small, voluntary food pantries, that's an American tragedy. It's the institutionalization of dependence, American style. A message that the government doesn't care." Betty Williams, who works with the Campaign for Family Stability, offered her own analysis. "It's a myth that people are hungry because they mismanage their money. The typical poverty family receives public assistance that's only forty-eight percent of the poverty level. You can't stretch forty-eight percent into one hundred percent." It was an inescapable fact that too many poor Chicagoans were trying to stretch too few dollars. At the time of our visit, approximately 20 percent of the city was living below the poverty line and another 20 percent just above it.

Throughout the day, other Task Force groups were fanning out across the city making site visits. Stanley Gershoff, Quentin Young, and Irwin Rosenberg, along with Sister Judy Bergen, spoke with unemployed steelworkers at their union headquarters and heard the now-familiar complaints: "We're angry and frustrated. U.S. Steel is shut down and Wisconsin Steel is on strike. They're putting on the pressure for us to take lower wages. The public aid system is demeaning, the administrators are unsympathetic and unresponsive. They're withholding food stamps from the strikers." At the Mary Magdalene food pantry, we heard the same litany of problems: no jobs, unsympathetic agency administrators, feeding programs not reaching hungry people because of bureaucratic red tape. "They're delaying certifying families for the school breakfast and lunch programs. Don't they know the children are hungry?"

Meanwhile, Gordon Harper had taken his group of doctors to visit a soup kitchen operated by the Missionaries of Charity, an order founded by Mother Teresa of Calcutta. Located in a church on the West Side, the enigmatic plaque outside the substantial brick building bore the names of Pope Leo and President Chester A. Arthur. The physicians stopped on the sidewalk to chat with a group of black men and women waiting their turn to enter the church basement to get a meal. It was nearly noon and most had not yet eaten that day. Gordon and his colleagues were ushered into the church by a young American sister dressed in a simple cotton sari. Inside some seventy people were filing past the food counter. On the wall a sign praised "Mary the Queen of Peace"; the guests spoke of needing jobs.

"The scene was, to me, very depressing," Gordon recounted. "The men seemed sullen and barely communicative, beaten down; all that against the spectacle of the Missionaries of Charity coming from Calcutta to the West Side of Chicago to provide food to the hungry." As the team moved on through Chicago's West Side ghetto they noted large areas that looked like a bombed-out city. Shells of abandoned buildings stood on lots where the debris had been left to remain.

The team's next stop was at the newly renovated headquarters of United Charities, where Reverend Hall had assembled a group of mothers who seemed fully aware of everything that was going wrong on the West Side: the fragmentation of community life, the predatory gangs operating at will in the neighborhood and, of course, hunger. "The gangs get money for the children so they can have food to eat," a mother pointed out. "We can barely afford to put food on the table, but the gangs can promise to take the kids to McDonald's."

The group had recently met with the Governor. After describing their problems, he said things would be changed so that no poor family in Illinois would get less than 54 percent of the federally calculated poverty standard. One of the mothers said angrily, "How can anyone expect families to cope with so little?"

Ida Carter, a forty-three-year-old head of a household of nine, spoke freely. "I live in a condemned building and pay two hundred and thirty-four of my three hundred and sixty-eight dollars in AFDC for rent. Four of the children have to sleep in one bed. I have diabetes and high blood pressure, and I've been in the hospital three times in the last year. I'm supposed to have a low-sodium diet. My son has asthma and congenital heart disease. We don't have enough to survive on. I can't afford to cook two meals a day. Some of my friends water down their medication so it will go farther."

The group's next stop was at Marillac House, a large Catholic settlement house on West Jackson Street, where they picked up local guides and visited a nearby public housing project. Inspecting the adjacent blocks, the physicians viewed the scatter of public-housing tenements amidst the devastation of many shattered brick buildings. Since the Great Chicago Fire, wood construction has not been permitted in the city, and one way for idle men to earn money has been to scavenge bricks from abandoned buildings. The bricks from the buildings were gone now, reducing the structures to their inner skeletons. A number of the scavengers, my colleagues learned, had died when buildings collapsed on them. Others had been arrested for trespassing.

The scenery around the projects was depressing: the grounds were covered with broken glass and litter, and one side of each building was now enclosed in heavy-gauge chain-link fencing, because furniture, refrigerators, and people had been thrown from the buildings' balconies. The outer doors to the apartments were fitted with accordion-style steel gates, the hallways filled with debris and the foul stench of urine.

As the group walked through the neighborhood, a nun leading their tour pointed out that "the elderly people live alone and have no cooking facilities whatsoever. An evening meal consists of a tin of cat food and a raw egg."

Cardinal Bernardin recently had visited the grim ghetto community and had been visibly shaken by what he saw. Sometime later a distinguished panel of Catholic bishops would deliver a scathing paper condemning the rise of poverty in America and calling for national action.

One of the doctors reported the experience had been terrifying. They had seen life on the edge, he said, a fragmented community of broken lives, high infant mortality, and government neglect. "Isn't this genocide?" he asked his colleagues.

"ECONOMIC RECOVERY IS ONLY A RUMOR HERE"

Our next destination was Peoria, a community that has always heralded itself as the All-American City. Located in the middle of Illinois, it lacks a seaport or major riverway that in earlier times might have formed the crossroads for commerce. Today, Peoria is surrounded by fields of corn and grain, seemingly endless acres planted by solid Midwestern families. Dotting the horizon are the church steeples and silos that mark the tallest structures, reminding the traveler of the institutions that bind the people.

Peoria also is the district of Congressman Robert Michel, at the time of our visit the Republican leader of the House of Representatives. As news signaled our visit, Michel's political opponents requested a meeting with our group. My staff agreed, provided it would be a public meeting and Mr. Michel participated as well. I wanted to keep our work clear from charges of partisanship.

Unfortunately, Michel did not agree to the meeting, although my staff spoke with his aides on numerous occasions. Each time the individual from his office would politely jot notes about our schedule and promise to call right back after speaking with the Congressman. But they never did.

A week before our departure for Illinois, I tried calling Mr. Michel, and a staff aide once again promised the Representative would promptly return my call. I then wrote Mr. Michel a personal note, inviting him to meet with us when we arrived in Peoria. Unfortunately, Congressman Michel never called back and did not answer my letter. As a result, we felt we had to cancel our meeting with the political leaders who had shown an interest in hunger.

Our first stop was the Peoria Salvation Army, where two young Midwesterners, John Colgan and John Arnold, briefed us on the unemployment situation. "At one time anyone who wanted a job could get one. But now thousands of breadwinners have been laid off and can't even find work at minimum wage. They've been laid off at the Caterpillar, Hiram Walker, and Pabst plants." In nearby Canton, they said, International Harvester had shut down completely, and coal mining had been dramatically cut back. Many people had given up and dropped out of the work force, no longer counted as unemployed.

"We hear rumors of economic recovery," Arnold said, "but I assure you that's not happening in Peoria."

Marjorie LaFont, a nurse with the Food and Nutrition Service, told of making home visits to some of the fifty thousand needy families in the area. "When I started back in 1972 we had to hunt to find hungry families. Today, we are overwhelmed. Taxpayers who worked to support assistance programs are now in line asking for help.

"I've seen malnourished children," LaFont went on, "whose conditions went unnoticed because their parents didn't have the money to take them to the doctor. About fifteen hundred children weren't allowed to start school last year because they didn't have the required school physical. The parents didn't have the money to spend on the doctor's visit. The teachers say they have hungry children in their classrooms all the time."

"FIVE THOUSAND HOMES FORECLOSED LAST YEAR"

We departed to see the children she described. At the home of Dorothy Davis, we met a grandmother raising the four children of her deceased daughter. Disabled and in failing health, Mrs. Davis was valiantly trying to support the four boys on a monthly income of less that $400 in public assistance and food stamps.

"My grandsons try to work some after school," she began proudly, "but it's not really much. With so much unemployment here it's hard for them to get work. The jobs are taken by men with families. Several days each month we are down to bread and water."

At the next house a mother told us candidly, "The last four years have been hell. I can't keep my eight-year-old daughter fed. I try hard to ration my food stamps but they just don't last."

"What kind of meals do you prepare?" I asked.

"Fresh vegetables, potatoes or rice, fish or hamburger, maybe a salad."

"That sounds like a nutritious diet," one of my colleagues said.

The mother looked at him in disbelief.

"Doctor, that's what I'd like to fix. Mostly we eat cornbread and beans."

And making more house calls, five of us headed off to the Labor Temple, a union hall in a small gothic building on a downtown side street. Inside were several dozen people who had come looking for work. Some inquired about obtaining public assistance because their unemployment benefits had run out.

"We thank you doctors for coming," the business manager said as he welcomed us, "for trying to understand the pain and suffering in our lives. The President's Task Force came here from Washington and it was a farce."

Several months before our arrival, members of President Reagan's Hunger Task Force had visited Peoria to determine if there was hunger. Erma Davis, a middle-aged black Peoria resident, had served on that panel and arranged the local visit. As the Director of the George Washington Carver Center, named after the famous black scientist who had found so many uses for peanuts, Ms. Davis was picked for her alleged knowledge of local conditions. Congressman Michel testified also, claiming that any existing problems in his district were disappearing by leaps and bounds as a result of Republican economics. In words that were reminiscent of what we had heard in Mississippi, many local residents had harsh criticism for the report of the Presidential panel, feeling that it was a whitewash of actual conditions.

Some expressed outright anger, while others spoke of the hopelessness and shame in being down-and-out. A neatly dressed thirty-three-year-old woman said, "I live with my son on an income of three hundred and sixty-eight dollars a month.

I don't like coming here to reveal my personal life in front of everyone." She glanced over to the press that had followed us. "But I got to because of my son. I'm willing to work. I always have. Just try me."

A fifty-three-year-old Army veteran sat nearby. "I was a painter, but I've been out of work for over two years." His tanned face and light hair reflected the Nordic features of many in the area. "I have no income, no car insurance, and my children study by candlelight because the electricity has been shut off. My wife and I frequently go hungry, the kids, too." He paused before finishing his comments. "I don't want to apply for food stamps. The politicians keep saying there aren't enough food stamps to go around. Maybe someone else needs them more than we do? I want to work. I keep hoping the phone will ring and someone will offer me a job." I gritted my teeth. Here was another decent man made to feel he should not be receiving public assistance even though his family was hurting so.

The momentary silence was broken as a woman suddenly stood, gesturing at the man beside her. "My husband has no work, but he's a good man. He's always provided for his family." The spouse she praised then spoke, but almost inaudibly. "When you are younger, you keep thinking you'll progress to middle-class. But, instead you get poorer. My mother went through the Depression and said things would be different for me. I know that somehow we've got to get through this."

"My mother sold her grave plots," announced a thirty-five-year-old man, whose pent-up feelings seemed to be released by the emotional outpouring of the others. "The plots keep her from qualifying for public assistance. She has no food. She sold the plots and lived off that for awhile. Then she ran out of the money." At this point, the young man stopped to collect his thoughts. "You know what happened?" he began again. "They said she was not qualified because you're not supposed to sell your assets to make yourself eligible."

The union business manager spoke up. "I keep files of our unemployed members. I have more than seven hundred files, mostly of families, where the breadwinner is out of work and the unemployment benefits have run out. They're still looking for work, but the government doesn't count them as unemployed because they've used up their benefits. . . . You take a young family around here. If they have no income they still can't get public assistance because they have a car, or maybe a house. Before they can become eligible for any help they have to sell them. There's no sense to government policies that run you into the ground before you can get help."

Here was the same story told again: government policies toward the poor failing to reflect a spirit of giving, of assisting people through hard times. There can be no rationale for a policy that penalizes an elderly woman for selling her grave plot, or that requires a young family to sell its only car in order to get help.

I recalled a conversation earlier that day at a feeding program for the elderly. A man in his mid-sixties, formerly employed by the Greater Peoria Mass Transit, had said, "I grew up in the Depression, but never dreamed I'd have to live like that again. My wife and I live with my retarded son. We get a little surplus cheese and butter from the government. We applied for food stamps, but get only seventeen dollars. . . . Our food stamps were cut down to seventeen dollars," he said, "when they put my son in a skill-training program for the handicapped. He's retarded. They cut the stamps by the amount of money he makes at the program. We can't get ahead."

At first I wondered whether I had heard him correctly, but the man's earnestness kept me from breaking into his story. "There's been too many helpful things cut out for me to believe that anyone cares. Our government doesn't show the principles of Christian love."

We made our way over to the Peoria public assistance

office, having been warned by our local guides that the director has a kind heart but a tough exterior. Looking at a picture on the wall of his office, I realized why Zack Monroe's name sounded familiar. His son, by the same name, had been a pitcher for the New York Yankees during the 1950s. Somewhere stored in my parents' home in Indiana was my stack of baseball cards with Zack Monroe among them. As we shook hands I noted that father and son looked a fair amount alike. I wondered what Zack Senior would have looked like in Yankee pinstripes.

Monroe's crustiness vanished when I asked him about his son's pitching. He also was frank about conditions in Peoria. "Things are getting worse, not better," he pointed out. "Even in the Depression there weren't as many people in need of help as now. It's discouraging to see families go broke when they have a forty-thousand-dollar house with only five thousand left on the mortgage. After all that hard work they lose the house. One mortgage company around here foreclosed on five thousand homes in the area last year."

Beneath the middle-class façade of the All-American city there was a lot of tragedy.

"Where Is All the Christianity?"

The early October evening was warm as people came to the church hall for our public hearing. Women wore sundresses and the men sported short-sleeved shirts. The style of their dress and the twang of their voices reminded us of our location in the heart of the Midwest.

First to testify was a woman who seemed to epitomize recent changes in the area. "I'm the daughter of farmers. I left the farm and came to the city eleven years ago to work at Caterpillar. A lot of people did that and were fine until a few years ago when we started losing jobs around here. Now we're losing our homes. Some of my friends are losing hope.

Sometimes I wonder, 'Where is all the Christianity I grew up learning about?' Where is all the wholesomeness I used to hear about?"

Hazel Martin took the opportunity to speak up. "I don't have a home. I lost it and had to move with the kids to a temporary shelter. I worked in a factory for ten years and then got laid off. When I applied for public assistance they told me I had to sell my car. That's not right. I worked in that factory and got scars and bruises for the things I had. It's mine and the government wants to take it away in order to get me some help. Why?"

In the Midwest the women often do most of the talking. In public forums the men slink back, shy and inarticulate, as though it is unmanly to reveal one's woes. Bill Davis broke the string of women speakers.

"I'm one of the 'new poor,'" he admitted. "I have six children. Both me and my wife worked for years until our plant closed. We take cold showers because the hot water heater broke and we don't have the money to buy another one. The roof leaks when it rains. We worry that the children don't get enough to eat." As he sat down his body language said, "No time for questions, I just wanted to tell someone what we've been going through."

The rolls at a local food pantry, we learned, were up more than 300 percent in three years. People told us that the pattern was similar for all the food pantries in the area.

Sixty-year-old Marge Singleton owns Sadie's Café on State Street. "I've been running Sadie's for seventeen years, and I'm in business to make money. But a lot of the time I just give out meals. I buy food for the old people. It breaks my heart to see people who've worked all their lives go hungry. They can't even die decently."

Donna Harrison spoke last. "I work for the Extension Service. I see a lot of hungry children. Even in our grade schools they are hungry. Some of them pick up leftover sandwiches from other kid's trays. . . . It's not only the children who are hurting, but their parents, too," she went on. "It's one thing to tell a child on Christmas that 'Santa didn't stop this year.' But, can you imagine the anguish of telling your child that you have no food for them?"

Hunger and poverty in Peoria were startling, in large part, because they were so unexpected. The Midwest has been synonymous with the bedrock of American life. Even the terms "heartland," "breadbasket," and "All-American City" seek to convey that image, which, in part, still exists. The hungry of Peoria have a veneer of comfort. Their clothes are not tattered; the homes look well-kept. Most families still have a car.

Yet, it is this veneer that makes the rise of the "new poor" in America's heartland so tragic. The appearances just do not match the reality of the circumstances, and when one looks at the acres and acres of fertile fields surrounding Peoria, it is all the more impossible to understand the unkept promise of prosperity amidst abundance.

"REALLY MISTER, HE'S NINE"

By the time we arrived in Missouri, the final leg of our odyssey, we were physically weary and emotionally drained by the grueling workdays and unremitting sight of severe hunger, poverty, and illness. One of our colleagues, in fact, dropped out of this final portion of the fieldwork, saying the schedule was too much for him. We wished each other well, all saddened by his premature departure.

Our launching point in Missouri would be Caruthersville, a town of nine thousand in the "Bootheel," named for the part of the state that protrudes into neighboring Arkansas. It is a rich and fertile plain whose main crops are soybeans, cotton, and rice. At the time of our visit, however, declining farm prices had devastated the already weak local economy and the region was suffering some of the worst poverty in the nation.

We became aware of the lingering history of racism in the

area as we stopped along a street to speak with residents of a black community. In a limousine, circling the block, was the white owner of the shacks housing local black families. He had come to see what the "strangers" were doing in town. It was not long before we realized the social climate in the area was not unlike that of much of the Deep South.

Our briefing in Caruthersville was led by Erma Moton, director of the Delta Ecumenical Ministries, a grass roots social-service organization serving the poor. As she described local conditions, her face grew stern. Then she focused on the mission at hand: "We just finished a dietary survey, and what I'm giving you is detailed information on hungry people right here in this community. We have names and addresses. You can visit these families yourself." She laid a pile of papers with data in front of me and said emphatically, "You can see, they don't eat much."

Later, we learned that our visit had not been the event to prompt the survey. Its genesis was more directly political and had been catalyzed by local issues. The Bootheel region forms the principal part of a congressional district represented by Republican Bill Emerson, a senior member of the House Select Committee on Hunger. Representative Emerson also sits on the House Agriculture Nutrition Subcommittee, which has jurisdiction over the food stamp program.

Prior to our visit Emerson had gone along with administration wishes and voted for massive cuts in federally sponsored nutrition programs. In public statements he had openly voiced skepticism that hunger was widespread in America, and he seemed equally oblivious to its presence in his district. Erma Moton and her colleagues had completed their survey to inform him of the facts, hoping that hard evidence would prompt their Representative to act. Unfortunately, Erma Moton's impressive efforts did not convince Emerson; later he would be a key proponent of a House bill to make additional cuts in the food stamp program. Fortunately for the poor, he would be on the losing side of the issue at that time.

After our briefing, we paid a visit to a Head Start program where the director minced no words. "Hunger for these kids is a common thing. I go into the homes and see how little food there is. Kids come into this program not knowing milk. Once in the program their little bodies seem to perk up, like that four-year-old over there." She pointed to one of the children. "When she came to us four months ago she was anemic."

Dolores Jones, a teacher in the program, joined our conversation as she poured juice into Dixie cups and handed the drinks to the snacking children. "You can't help but notice that they come back to school in the fall having lost weight." Somewhat defensively Mrs. Jones added, "The parents aren't bad, they just don't have the money."

We arrived at the town hall by early afternoon to find a long line of people waiting in the hot sun for government-surplus cheese. Old and young, black and white, they had begun lining up at seven forty-five that morning. We walked along the line of waiting recipients, engaging them in conversation and learning about their circumstances.

Three older women stood together chatting. "I've been waiting for two hours," a seventy-one-year-old woman said, clutching a small cloth bag to carry the cheese. She spoke frankly, "I live on social security and it's not enough."

"How old are you, ma'am?" I asked, turning to one of her companions.

"Sixty-one. My doctor told me I shouldn't be eatin' starches, but I got to." She is a diabetic, she explained, but starchy food is all she could afford. She ate vegetables only three or four times a month. I learned that the third of the trio, an eighty-nine-year-old, also was on a diet. "I've got sickle cell. The doctor told me I should be eatin' liver, beets, carrots, and fruit. But, I got about two hundred dollars a month to live on, so's I can't buy those things, like I should."

Nearby, a very obese woman stood with her two children, ages six and eight.

"What do you do?" I inquired.

"I worked most of my life," she answered. "When the mobile home factory was goin' I worked there. I also worked pickin', you know, migrant work in the fields." The family received food stamps but they did not last the month. The mother said her children sometimes go hungry, "mainly livin' on beans, cornbread 'n potatoes."

Further down the line I heard someone raising his voice to one of my colleagues. I excused myself and walked over, hoping it was not a serious conflict. "Do you think I'd stand in line all day for some cheese if I wasn't hungry?" an elderly man yelled. "Meese says I'm a cheat. He should come down here and stand in this hot sun and then call us cheats."

The sun was hot as we left the town, and our reprieve was to be the shade afforded by Effie Alsop's front porch. Her wrinkled white face showed the wear of her eighty-six years. She lead us inside, where we began to chat.

"Ms. Alsop," I asked, "could you tell us what you've been eating?"

"I haven't had nothin' yet today."

With some persistence, one of my colleagues learned that she had not eaten for about twenty-four hours. We asked again if she was hungry. "I get hungry when I got food in the house. But, when I don't have none I don't seem to get hungry. Isn't that funny, doctor?"

Effie Alsop's husband, also in his eighties, took me into the kitchen. I looked into the cupboard and the refrigerator, finding some dried white beans in a glass jar and several pieces of bread in the refrigerator.

"How often do you eat fruits and vegetables?" I queried. Mr. Alsop simply shook his head, dismissing a question whose answer was obvious.

"Do you and your wife ever go a day without eating?" I followed.

"Yes sir, I'd say at least several days every month."

After speaking with the Alsops, my team split up to make house calls. In a nearby community I visited Mrs. Spain, whose younger black face contrasted sharply with Effie Alsop's wrinkles.

"I've got five children," she said proudly, showing off two well-groomed youngsters. "Yolanda here is two and Natasha is five. The others are in school."

"My husband is out lookin' for work," she reported. "But, there's nothin' aroun'. It's a full-time job just lookin' for work aroun' here." Mr. Spain had lost his job several months before. The family lived on $269 a month. There would have been nine to feed, but two of their daughters had died in a fire the previous year.

I asked permission to look into the refrigerator, where I found eight hot dogs, four peppers, a carton of milk, and some eggs.

"Do you ever run out of milk for the children?" I asked.

"All the time," she responded.

Something prompted me to push a little farther. "What would you do, if you ran out of food altogether?" Her quick response told me she had already asked herself the same question. "I'd march them to the grocery store, sit them down on the floor and give them food. At least they couldn't arrest me for stealing."

Out on the sidewalk I saw a cute little boy who responded with a smile as I playfully tugged on his ear. Judging from his size, he looked about six years old.

"What's your name?" I asked.

"Lee."

"How old are you?"

"Nine."

Knowing that young children sometimes inflate their age, I laughed and turned to his older sister.

"How old is your brother, really?"

"Really mister, he's nine."

I tried as inconspicuously as possible to signal Naomi Kistin to come over, wanting to rely on her pediatric eye to determine whether Lee could possibly be nine years old.

Naomi took a look at Lee and brought him into his mother's house. I spoke with the mother while Naomi examined Lee in the living room. "The doctor at the clinic said he's anemic," Lee's mother confessed. "I know what he should be eatin', but I just can't buy it," she added. "My husband's been tryin' to find work, but there's nothin' around here for him."

Lee's father, Robert, a man of thirty-five, joined the conversation. "We can't get no help 'cause I live here with my family. They could get if it I left, but we want to keep the family together."

"What do you want?" I asked.

"A job, a steady job. Just the opportunity to prove myself," he said.

As we walked to the car, Naomi said that little Lee seemed to be suffering from growth failure. The actual unemployment rate in the area, we had been told, was around 30 percent of the able-bodied work force, so it seemed unlikely that Robert would find work to bring home more food for his undersized son.

"SOMETHING MAGICAL SHOULD HAVE HAPPENED BY NOW"

The remainder of the day my colleagues and I spent in nearby back-road communities. In the tiny hamlet of Hayti, the health center director described how their slots for the WIC program had been cut back, forcing them to drop some of the high-risk children from the program. To offset the impact of the budget cuts, the center had opened an emergency food distribution program. Although clearly still an unorthodox practice, by now it was not uncommon to hear of health facilities taking up the task of giving out food. "No one else around here is doing it," the director continued. "We're just about out of resources, but we're doing the best we can."

Meanwhile, Gordon Harper had taken another team to Washington County, an area of lead and barite mines to the north of Caruthersville. Settled by French farmers in the eighteenth century, the county is now officially one of the poorest in the nation. The mines are shut down; unemployment is very high.

Prior to our visit, Catholic workers in Washington County had reported that hunger was a very serious problem, and our doctors wished to see for themselves. Traveling with priests from St. Joachim's Church, they walked down dirt roads and hopped across streams to visit homes. They found living conditions reminiscent of Appalachia: families living in rusty trailers off to the side of small clearings, scrawny dogs running alongside children who hauled water in empty lard cans.

The Eckhoff family, seven children, wife, and husband, lived in one of those small trailers. Next door sat another trailer, rusted out, and slowly being cannibalized for firewood and building materials. Insulation and wiring could be seen through holes in the walls. Inside the Eckhoff's small living area was a lightweight wood stove that had cost about $60 and was not expected to last another winter.

Lillian Eckhoff pointed to the three-year-old and said, "She's the sickly un'. If she ain't got a cold she's got diarrhea."

Mr. Eckhoff had been disabled in a mining accident years before and was now unable to work. Despite his disability, he was ineligible for SSI, and the family was living primarily on food stamps. "About all we can get with them is milk and hash."

Stopping briefly at other homes, the doctors followed a long dirt road into the woods to find the residence of a black family. Their compound was a series of filthy wood shacks lacking utilities, with chickens roaming about. The guide explained, "There are very few black families in this county. The few who are here are left over from slavery days. Many white families make it clear they'd like to drive them out."

The ceilings of the shacks were so low that the visitors had to stoop to enter. The matriarch, a woman with an enormous goiter, proudly showed three framed documents: a wedding license from the 1920s, a 1924 certificate for attendance in the eighth grade, and a graduation certificate. By completing requirements for the eighth grade, she had been granted a diploma that read, "Entitled to enroll in any high school in the State of Missouri." Before the words "high school" was inserted the word "colored."

As Gordon's team drove away one of the priests told of a family nearby who had been visited by a fellow Brother weighing about three hundred pounds. The large Friar had arrived as they were sitting down to dinner. The mother insisted that he share the little food they had. "In the mythologies and in the Bible," the priest said, "something magical should happen to change their fortunes for the better. It should have happened by now," he sighed, "but it hasn't."

We left that evening for Cape Girardeau, from which we would catch a flight to St. Louis the next morning. Before retiring the twelve members of our team met for a discussion over a dinner of chicken and ribs. Away from the press and public, we let our hair down, telling humorous stories and recounting events that helped to release tension and assuage depression. I think we were fully aware of the irony of our momentary pleasure amidst the sadness we felt, but we chose not to talk about it.

"WE HAD TO LOCK THE GARBAGE BINS"

The next morning we had no time to check in at our hotel, so, luggage in hand, we dashed into three taxi cabs and headed for our first appointment of the day—in a St. Louis slum. "Look for a man with a dashiki, beads, and a smile," I had been told by my staff. "His name is Otis Woodward, and he'll stand out in any crowd." Woodward, a Luthern family outreach worker, was scheduled to be one of our local guides.

While we sipped coffee and ate donuts in the large warehouse of the St. Louis Food Crisis Network, Woodward described our itinerary for the day. "There is a hidden America

An elderly woman tells Dr. Deborah Frank (*center right*), "I can't afford rent, utilities, and food. All I have at home is Wonder Bread, government cheese, and Tang." Elderly Feeding Program, Rhode Island.   (*Physician Task Force on Hunger*)

We found the resources of the food pantries and soup kitchens stretched to the limit. William Woodside, president of the American Can Company, pointed out, "Government created hunger, and only the government can solve it." New England food pantry.   (*Physician Task Force on Hunger*)

We found growing numbers of children eating in the soup kitchens of New England. "This is our only full meal for today," a mother tells one of our doctors. Massachusetts soup kitchen. (Greenfield Recorder, *Greenfield, Massachusetts*)

As the government proposed to cut nutrition programs for the elderly, Drs. Gordon Harper and Bill Beardslee learned that this woman crawls on her hands and knees to get to her garden. "I rely on what I grow," she said. Greenwood, Mississippi. (*Tom Powell, Mississippi Governor's Office*)

We saw more empty refrigerators than any of us care to remember. This family's food stamps had run out, and they had no way to buy food for the next week. The Mississippi Delta. *(Tom Powell, Mississippi Governor's Office)*

The hole in this child's room was stuffed with old clothing last winter. In our travels, we learned that the hungry lack for most of life's necessities.
(Steve Haines, The Providence Journal-Bulletin)

One of our doctors remarked that the poverty we saw in Mississippi reminded him of his native South Africa. After seeing McClure's Alley, we believed him. Greenwood, Mississippi. (*Steve Haines,* The Providence Journal-Bulletin)

A father holds his child and worries how he will be able to feed his family. In the Deep South, we found high infant mortality rates and inadequate nutrition. Greenwood, Mississippi.
(*Steve Haines,* The Providence Journal-Bulletin)

This eighty-one-year-old woman sews bonnets to supplement her income. "My social security just ain't enough," she confides to our doctors. They found that her cupboards were bare. Nashville, Tennessee. (*Kathleen Smith, Nashville, Tennessee*)

Dr. Tom Yeager and Dr. Larry Brown learn that for many children the meals provided at this day-care center will be their only ones for the day. Nashville, Tennessee. (*Kathleen Smith, Nashville, Tennessee*)

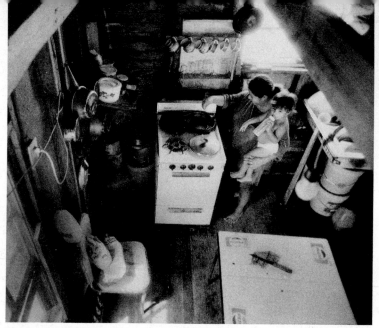

This Texas child consumes fewer vitamins and calories than necessary for optimal growth. "The parents know what to buy," a local nutritionist told us, "but they can't afford it." Rio Grande Valley, Texas.

(*Steve Haines*, The Providence Journal-Bulletin)

This Chicago family walked two miles to get to the food pantry at St. Luke's Lutheran Church. At the time of our visit, 20 percent of Chicago's population was living below the poverty line and as many more were just above it. Chicago, Illinois. (*Steve Haines*, The Providence Journal-Bulletin)

Families like this one were losing their farms throughout the Midwest. The safety net of social programs was not there to support these once-proud people. Revillo, South Dakota. (*Steve Haines*, The Providence Journal-Bulletin)

This Arkansas couple is one of several million families that the federal food stamp program fails to reach. "We get pretty low sometimes," they admitted. Ozark Mountains. (*Steve Haines*, The Providence Journal-Bulletin)

Seven million citizens participated in "Hands Across America," joining these people in Washington, D.C., to call for an end to domestic homelessness and hunger. (*USA for Africa*)

waiting to be seen," he warned. "We're pleased that you have come to see what we see every day." Woodward told us that we would see the "unseen and uncounted," the old people who never come out of their little apartments, the men living beneath the stairwells, the little children nobody thinks about. "Many of them will tell you they're okay. They'll show you the best room in their house. They have pride. But they're hungry and they're poor."

We filed out of the warehouse and hopped into waiting cars; the press followed in their vans. The first stop was at the Darst-Webbe Housing Project, a series of red brick buildings that looks like any other large housing project built in the 1950s. Huge green garbage bins fenced off the asphalt streets and sidewalks. Our destination was the Catholic Guardian Angel Center, operating out of one end of the project. When they first opened the Center the volunteers passed out free bread every day. Soon there were too many mouths to feed, so they started a food pantry.

Evelyn Webb, who administers the program, told us that area residents, many of whom are poor themselves, donate tinned goods and other items for the hungry. "Some people donate water because they have little else to give," she said. "There are people in nearby houses who have no utilities, no food." Webb paused to ponder the implications of her next point. "Things keep getting worse. We just had to put more secure locks on the garbage bins so the mothers and children couldn't raid the receptacles at night. We didn't want them getting sick on the rotted food."

Across town we ate lunch with soup kitchen guests in the basement of Our Savior Luthern Church. Max Pepper, a transplanted New Yorker who now chairs the Department of Community Medicine at St. Louis University Medical School, sat across the table from me and talked with a young family. Daniel Lukins, a tall man with a quiet Southern accent, held his four-year-old daughter, Regina. His wife ate by their side. I marveled at the ease with which Max struck up a conversation: a short, Jewish physician, prominent in his field, and a young black man from the rural South enjoying each other's company in this most unusual environment.

"I'm a cook and I've been out of work for four months," Lukins confided. "When the unemployment checks stopped we got into trouble. We had no food, so we started coming here for one meal a day. Today, we didn't have anything for breakfast and my little girl has been hungry. This will be our only meal today."

"Regina has had some health problems," Mrs. Lukins said. "I'm not exactly sure what is wrong, because I haven't taken her to the doctor. We used to pay five dollars for the visit, but the government has changed things and it costs nineteen dollars. We just can't pay that kind of money now." Max directed them to a clinic at his hospital and said he would help them.

Mr. Lukins summed up the plight of his family. "You hear all these campaign promises to make life better. Then they get in and we are told to keep this thirty-pound weight on our backs for the rest of our lives."

I went over to chat with fifty-one-year-old Mrs. Love, who sat in the corner of the hall having a donut and coffee. She said that she had worked for many years as a hotel maid—until a bus accident crushed her foot. After the accident she was denied disability and now lived on $146 a month, half of it in food stamps. Her apartment had no heat.

"How long since you've eaten?" I inquired.

"Just yesterday."

"And today? What have you had?"

"Four donuts and two salads. Here," she added.

"Are there ever days when you go without food?"

"I've been days without food. I get headaches, but they go away if I get something to eat."

"And when you don't get something to eat?"

"Know what I do, doctor? I get me some water and I put sugar in it and I drink it. That helps."

My hand moved out to sit atop hers as we talked. I was imagining her day-to-day existence and not retaining all she was saying; my pen and notepad lay still on the table while my mind wandered. Mrs. Love said something about losing weight which brought back my concentration.

"How much weight have you lost?" I asked.

"Since I been most hungry, about one hundred pounds."

"Empty Baskets Waiting for Food"

From Our Savior we pushed on with local guides to visit more soup kitchens. At Notre Dame Parish we spoke with church workers who had begun a food pantry. "We started seeing so many families new to poverty and hunger that we had to do something," one of the priests explained. "The General Motors plant laid off many employees, a number of them even lost their homes."

Beulah Campbell, the full-blooded Cherokee woman who operates the facility, confirmed the priest's words. "Everyone comes here: women, children, the elderly. We doubled the number of people we served in the first year. There's a sense of hopelessness. No matter what people do, the pit gets deeper. If a family makes an extra ten or fifteen dollars a month, the government deducts it from their assistance. It's discouraging, you know." At St. Patrick's Center one of the nuns spoke eloquently about the sense of discouragement that hits people who cannot find work. "The unemployed who come in every day to look at job listings find that the labor pool for the day fills up quickly. The people left are a residue of willing bodies and discouraged spirits."

Off in the reception area sat several men, each hoping that the telephone would ring to offer a job. Sixty-year-old Mr. Griffith sat silently, until I placed myself next to him and opened up the conversation.

"What do you do, sir?" I began.

"I'm in the engineering business. Well, I mean I graduated with a Master's in Engineering from Tulane about twenty years ago." He had run a chain of convenience stores for the last eighteen years. The chain went out of business; bankruptcy wiped out his pension, and Griffith had nothing to show for his years of work.

"How about your family?" I asked to change the subject.

"My wife and daughter were killed in an automobile accident. I have a daughter and son-in-law who live in another state. I have a granddaughter, too." The family did not know he was out of work. He thought they would worry and knew they had to support themselves. Meanwhile he lived on hope that things would change. "I wanted to work it out 'til I was sixty-five and retired, but I didn't make it. There's not a lot for men like me, even though I feel like I can work and contribute."

I moved on to talk with other men, all sitting quietly, until one inquired whether a new job order had come in. Ron Cannon, a youthful-looking man from New Orleans, said he had looked for carpentry work for six months. "After that I was willing to take anything, even a dishwasher's job." He paused as I tried to accommodate myself to his heavy drawl. "Why can't the government do something like the CCC?" he asked, referring to one of the Depression-era employment programs of the Roosevelt administration. "I want to work; others do, too. I was out on the street at five o'clock this morning selling papers to motorists going to work."

Sandwiched between the men sat Mrs. Anderson, a fifty-nine-year-old cook. "I have a job. I cook from seven in the morning 'til one in the afternoon. Sometimes I can get work cleaning offices from four in the afternoon to about ten in the evening." When I questioned her she said she had no choice but to hold down two jobs. "There just isn't enough to buy food if I don't. When I run out of milk for my grandchild, that's when I get worried the most."

At the Salvation Army Children's Center the staff said that feeding problems "are prominent among the children who come here. About half of them are below the fifth percentile for size. Some seem to take no pleasure from eating and avoid eye contact while they eat, others eat voraciously. Many come here in the winter because their homes lack heat as well as food."

A St. Louis County social worker said that children are being referred for foster care because the parents can't provide enough food. In the winter this can mean twenty-five to thirty additional placements a month. "One family we have here," the social worker said, "just had their kids taken away because they had no food. The parents came to the shelter for help. It took us a month to get the kids back. The father is a master chef who worked for twenty-five years."

At the New Life emergency food distribution facility, Gordon Harper met a fifty-seven-year-old woman with a twelve-year-old son. "I look for day work," she said, "but I can't find it. We need dental care but the free clinic costs five dollars a visit. We were out of food and told to come here." Two weeks earlier their apartment had been broken into. "The burglars stole a radio, shoes, and food. They went into the refrigerator and took cheese, green beans, stewed tomatoes, franks, even dog bones that were wrapped in foil."

In the nearby town of LeMay, Stan Gershoff's team visited a working-class community. From January to September 1984 the facility provided groceries for approximately three thousand families, nearly ten thousand people in all, of whom 38 percent of the adults were unemployed. Since the total population of the community is only fifty-three thousand, it meant that slightly under 20 percent of the community was relying on emergency food assistance.

Others of us, meanwhile, were visiting with medical staff at the People's Clinic. Nearly three-fourths of their patients were living in poverty, they said, and many were hungry. "I frequently find female patients with blisters around their mouths," one doctor said. "Many eat little besides cereal. You can see the malnutrition on their faces. Around the third week of the month the food stamps run out. Patients come in asking for work to do. We provide food like we provide medicine."

"We see quite a bit of growth failure among our pediatric population," one of the nurses affirmed. "Just this morning two parents brought their eleven-month-old child in because she was not gaining weight. Their electricity had been shut off for over a year and they had been feeding the baby only formula." Another nurse reported that parents ask if their children might have a glass of milk from the clinic refrigerator, or if they might have some bread. "It's odd being trained in medicine," she said, "and spending so much time simply trying to feed our patients."

We ended our visit to St. Louis with a public hearing at the Soldier's Memorial. It was with some relief that we prepared for the event. Although we were tired and felt we had seen enough, in a strange way we had grown fond of the exhausting work and the people we had met.

First to speak was Edie Mae Binyoun, a middle-aged woman who announced that she had a Ph.D. degree in poverty. "I earned it over the last twenty years. P is for poverty. H is for hell and hunger. D is for determination. I'm a mother of three, one child is epileptic. I have high blood pressure, and I've had a stroke. Life hasn't been easy for me or my children, but each day I hope that it will improve."

Reverend Larry Rice pointed to the irony in holding a hunger hearing at a memorial to the war dead. "We spend money on weapons while the real 'soldiers' die in the streets of this city. . . . Our church gives frozen food away to keep it from spoiling. I've seen people tear it open on the sidewalk and eat it still frozen. They couldn't wait until they got it home."

At this point Reverend Rice raised his voice in passion. "You've heard that people here eat out of trash cans. What you need to know is how they fight to do it. How they fight over control of the dumpsters. . . . We've got a very serious problem in this country," he concluded. "Government leaders and corporations either want to ignore the need, or deal only with the symptom and not the cause."

I thought his reference to "people dying in the streets" a bit melodramatic, but Monsignor Shockley of the St. Louis Archdiocese took up the point. A graying man in a clerical collar, he declared, "Men come to the city hospital emergency room and collapse on the floor. Not because they are sick, but because they are hungry. Why should something so important as food be dependent on charity? We don't tell people they can't have air or water, or that they'll have them only twenty days a month," the Monsignor went on, drawing an obvious parallel to food stamps that never last the month. "Why do we do it with food?"

Volunteers who run emergency feeding programs had come to describe their efforts to obtain nutritious food. "In St. Louis, local industries make donations to food banks and soup kitchens," a worker testified. "Much of it is junk, insofar as nutritional standards go." Some of it is junk according to *any* standards, we had found. Industries often donate rotten produce, making the most of their civic endeavors by taking a tax deduction for food they cannot sell.

With our work concluded, the twelve of us headed for the airport. We were off to our respective homes in nine different states, a bit tired and overwhelmed and anxious to resume our lives.

We had come to the breadbasket of America—the world's most prolific agricultural region—and found substantial hunger. It was not difficult to find. One could see it in the homes of poor neighborhoods, in inner-city health centers, in shelters for the homeless and, of course, at the soup kitchens.

We had seen children who were not growing and had talked with unemployed parents who worried about their inability to feed their babies. We had found elderly people living on rice or beans, and for periods of time, on nothing at all.

As I headed off to the airport, someone handed me a document that I stuffed into my briefcase. Opening it later on the plane, I saw it was a report on hunger in the small city of Warrensberg, just outside Kansas City. The study had been conducted by a professor at Central Missouri State University, and the commentary at the end of the paper caught my eye:

> *As we sit above the caves filled with the government stored food, and as we shudder at the nuclear warheads implanted in our fields, we are faced with the travesty that even in the Breadbasket of America there are empty baskets waiting for food.*

6

Stalking a Disease to the
White House

AFTER more than two years of field investigations in diverse regions of the nation, we had reached a shocking conclusion. *At least twenty million Americans were going hungry at some time each month,* a level of human misery reminiscent of the Great Depression. Equally distressing, we had uncovered overwhelming evidence that this hunger was a man-made epidemic created and spread by government policies.

As the media followed us around the country we were asked again and again what we would do with the information we were collecting. Our answer was always the same. We intended to write a report and present it to the American people and the Congress. We would describe what we had found; the rest would be up to the nation.

On New Year's Day, 1985, my staff and I began a process that would consume weekdays and weekends, working days and evening hours. We integrated hundreds of pages of notes from the investigating doctors, an even greater quantity of public testimony, the results of studies, and volume after volume of government documents. Chapters were drafted and sent to Task Force colleagues for review and rewriting. Meetings were held, additional data were obtained, computer programs were run. The pressure rose each time members of Congress called to inquire about our progress, or the press to scoop our findings. For a harrowing six weeks the distinction between night and day became relatively meaningless. All who participated in the work deserve extraordinary praise for their effort and professionalism; I do not remember a single complaint about the long hours or the utterance of an unkind or frustrated word about the pace.

"THE VENEER OF CIVILIZATION HAS WORN VERY THIN"

On February 12, all came to fruition in a crowded conference room at the headquarters of the American Public Health Association in Washington, D.C. Before some fifteen television crews and a hundred members of the national press, my colleagues and I presented our findings to the public. Also staring us in the face was the correspondent from Tass, the Soviet news agency, who produced in us the unsettling emotion of bringing America's hunger crisis into the arena of the Cold War. Later that day, we held a second press conference in the more comfortable and familiar environment of the Harvard School of Public Health. It was a homecoming of sorts, presided over by Dean Harvey Fineberg, who held a copy of our report in hand and described the specter of hunger in our nation as a "moral outrage."

That evening, the national network news carried the story at the top of the hour: "A national team of prominent physicians affiliated with Harvard University reports that twenty million Americans are hungry." I watched the broadcast with disbelief as a White House spokesman refused comment, stonewalling with the excuse that no one in the Reagan Administration had seen the report as yet—although we had hand-delivered a dozen copies to the White House the previous day and had received written confirmation on their arrival.

Later, a spokesman for the Department of Agriculture, which oversees most federal food programs, flatly disagreed with our findings. "The problem of hunger is not widespread," he declared, though we had documented its existence in every region of the nation. "The federal government is doing more to end hunger than any administration in recent history," he concluded, even though we had seen firsthand the devastating effects of sharp federal cutbacks and mean-spirited regulations.

The administration's Big Lie left us stunned and disappointed. Each of us had hoped that our report would spark an honest, open, and bipartisan look at hunger in America.

The next evening, the networks did a follow-up on the story. Anchorman Dan Rather, in a commentary on CBS, responded to the administration's contention that our statistics were wrong with a rhetorical question, "Let's say the Harvard study is off by nineteen million. Would we be proud of a nation that has one million hungry people?"

On NBC, John Chancellor commented that our report reflected on America itself, saying, "Is the United States becoming a country in which most people have theirs and nobody bothers about those who don't have enough—a power abroad with an epidemic at home? With twenty million Americans who don't have enough [to eat] the veneer of civilization seems to have worn very thin."

It was especially distressing that the administration took issue with our figures, which we had been so careful to state conservatively. Just a short time before, pollster Louis Harris had conducted a nationwide survey, concluding that some twenty-one million Americans were periodically going hungry. And a variety of other analysts agreed with our estimates.

The debate on the numbers served only to obfuscate the real issue: Americans were going hungry while the country's leaders turned away from their suffering.

Gary Trudeau captured the frustration we felt in one of his *Doonesbury* comic strips. While Michael stares into the television set and eats a sandwich, the announcer blares, "The problem of twenty million hungry Americans was in the news briefly today." In the final frame Michael looks bewildered as the announcer adds, "But only briefly."

Meanwhile, Massachusetts Senator Edward Kennedy and Representative Barney Frank distributed copies of our study to members of Congress. Shortly thereafter, a House Agriculture subcommittee, chaired by Democrat Leon Panetta of California, arrived in Boston to hold hearings. Missouri Congressman Bill Emerson, who served on the Agricultural Committee and whose Congressional district we had visited, participated as well, making it clear he disapproved of our conclusions. Even as he admitted that he had not read the report, Emerson dismissed it as "Too much heat and too little light. The federal government," he added, "is doing about all it can. The private sector needs to step in to help."

We had found the resources of the private, voluntary agencies already stretched to the limit. Emerson clearly had not listened to the food pantry and soup kitchen workers in his own district or anywhere else. Nor was he being realistic about the desire or ability of large corporations to take on the job of feeding America's hungry.

"What we need is leadership that transcends ideology," I said in answer. "Our nation once ended hunger, and we can do it again if our leaders lead."

Bill Emerson, I would learn later, has a softer, more sensitive interior that is covered by his combative crust. In more cordial follow-up conversations, I would find him to be a decent man who goes to church and cares about family and friends. Nevertheless, he staunchly favors a minimal role for government in alleviating social problems. Two years later, we would meet again in his Washington office and he would reiterate the Reagan Administration line that "we should not throw money at problems."

"You don't seem to mind spending billions for defense," I pointed out, "sometimes pouring dollar after dollar for weapons that fail and can't be made to work. It's only when it comes to helping the poor and hungry that you want the government to take a back seat." It was clear we did not see eye to eye.

"GOVERNMENT CREATED HUNGER, ONLY GOVERNMENT CAN SOLVE IT"

Our report did not stop at documenting the existence of hunger, but went on to describe why and how it had so swiftly returned to haunt the land. We also put forth suggestions as to what we, as a nation, could do about it. Aaron Shirley voiced the feelings of Task Force members when he said, "As doctors, our job isn't merely to tell the patient he is sick. We have to tell him why he is sick and what we can do together to help get him well again."

Without doubt, the underlying cause of the disease was that the patient was not well to begin with. America's safety net for the poor was weaker than any of us had realized— much weaker than the networks that exist in most other industrialized nations in the world. Virtually no other modern nation permits the gaps in meeting basic human needs that we do. By almost any measure, from family health care to hospital coverage, from food assistance to income supports, from job security to day care, poor Americans are more vulnerable than their counterparts in industrialized nations that have fewer resources than we do. In the area of health care, for example, only two modern nations have no system of national health insurance: the United States and South Africa.

Perhaps in no area, however, is the fundamental weakness of America's safety net so apparent as that of assistance to families who become destitute. We were shocked at what we learned, and we still believe that other citizens will be shocked if they know the facts.

Many of the poorest, most vulnerable families in the United States receive no help at all. Contrary to popular belief, which is fostered by politically motivated rhetoric, most of the poor in the nation either receive no governmental assistance, or receive amounts so paltry as to make it impossible to maintain the health and dignity of the family.

In over half the states, for example, an unemployed family with two parents and children is not entitled to public assistance, no matter how penniless they may be. The Aid to Families with Dependent Children (AFDC) program was established by Congress to help American families during times of economic hardship. Yet the federal government left to the states the decision of whether to extend the program's protection to families when the father is in the home. Because of financial considerations, the majority of states do not assist such families, no matter how deserving and how destitute they may be. The father must leave the home before the AFDC program can be used to help the family. We had met such fathers during our travels around the nation, men who had been decent breadwinners and kind parents, who were driven to "desert" their families to help them through temporary periods of unemployment.

Impoverished families in many states are denied medical coverage as well. Again, it does not matter how destitute they may be. About a quarter of the states provide no Medicaid coverage to medically needy families; still other states provide no medical and no welfare assistance for childless couples and single individuals, even if they are penniless.

For poor Americans who are fortunate enough to receive some help during times of trouble, the assistance they get is grossly inadequate. The two basic programs designed to help families are AFDC and food stamps. Perhaps the most generous "welfare program," AFDC provides contemptibly little to a family of four: the average monthly grant is $91 in Mississippi, $177 in North Carolina, $247 in Missouri, $463 in Massachusetts, and $660 in California. Most states provide grants for four-person families in the vicinity of $300 to $400 monthly. Sometimes the grants go higher, yet these are the average grants for the states. Any parent who considers the cost of housing, food, medical care, clothing, education, and general upkeep can imagine how inadequate this most basic and most generous program really is. Some people who do not get AFDC get state relief, usually provided at one-third to one-half of the AFDC allotment.

When faced with evidence of the obvious inadequacy of these benefits, some politicians respond that the figures fail to take into account the benefits of food stamps. According to current government reports, slightly more than half the poor in America receive food stamps. Or, to put it another way, nearly half the citizens our government knows are living below the poverty level are *not* being helped by the food stamp program. Families fortunate enough to get food stamps receive an average benefit of forty-nine cents per person for each meal. This comes to less than $45 a month. By no stretch of the imagination can children be raised on such an amount, even if the family also receives AFDC.

The food stamp budget is an example of bureaucracy gone awry. The allotment is not based on nutritional studies of human need. Instead, a computer was programmed to take a predetermined budget and design a food stamp plan equal to that amount. When the plan was devised, nutritionists within the U.S. Department of Agriculture, which runs the program, warned that it would be nutritionally inadequate over extended periods of time. Not surprisingly, the USDA's own studies show that in over 80 percent of households living on the basic food stamp expenditure people fail to obtain recommended minimal dietary allowances for nutrients.

Some have argued that this failure is because food stamp recipients do not make wise purchases, that they waste money on expensive items of junk food. Here, too, the facts help us separate out the fancy. USDA studies consistently show that poor Americans make wiser purchasing choices than do the rest of us. They make their food dollar stretch farther. These studies reflect common sense: if you do not have a lot to spend, you watch how you spend it.

One of the reasons that AFDC and food stamp benefits are so inadequate is that they have not been indexed to keep up with inflation. This is especially true of AFDC, where grant levels, if adjusted for inflation, dropped 33 percent from 1970 to 1984. This means that a typical family today has one-third less purchasing power from an AFDC grant than in 1970. It is as if social security recipients did not get cost-of-living increases each year tied to inflation. Their grants would remain the same, but what they could buy would diminish by a third.

This loss in real income is not merely the result of unintended consequences. Starting out with a safety net already more fragile than similar nations, the United States has permitted its most vulnerable people—primarily families with children—to suffer even more greatly.

As this trend was taking place, a second factor—recession, with its economic dislocation, increasing unemployment, and skyrocketing poverty—came into play. Even today, although double-digit inflation and unemployment have diminished, the purchasing power of low- and medium-income households remains virtually unchanged.

In the early years of the decade, unemployment rose to the highest levels since the Great Depression. Long-term unemployment rates, measuring people out of work six months or more, rose dramatically. Going into 1985, long-term unemployment was up 70 percent over what it had been in 1980. And there is still more to consider. The government reports numbers of "discouraged workers" differently from the long-term unemployed. The discouraged are those who have been out of work so long they have given up looking for a job. This category rose to 1,300,000 in 1984, an increase of nearly 25 percent over 1980. Some of these workers were among the

5.1 million Americans who had their jobs abolished in recent years.

Many of us, no doubt, think we have protection against unemployment through the unemployment insurance program. But many of today's unemployed find this protection to be elusive. Of the eight million people out of work in late 1984, only 2.9 million received unemployment benefits. Due to the length of the recession and federal policies, the program had become so weak that as of early 1986 only 25 percent of jobless Americans received any unemployment compensation. This means that in more than half the states of this nation, an unemployed breadwinner living with spouse and children is unlikely to receive any unemployment benefits, AFDC, or Medicaid.

America's weakened safety net and the sagging economy thus came together to produce poverty unprecedented in two decades. About twenty-six million Americans lived in poverty in 1979. By 1983 that number had risen to more than thirty-four million, and it remained over thirty-three million through the end of 1985.

The most striking thing about the stunning increase in poverty is the sheer number of people in this country who live below the minimum level which the government itself determines necessary to raise a family—around $11,000 for a family of four. Most impoverished families have income closer to *half* that amount.

Also striking is who lives in poverty. Twenty years ago, the elderly comprised a large proportion of the poor in America. But the social security program was improved, and today the elderly poor constitute a much smaller percentage of the destitute in this nation. Children have replaced the elderly as the poorest group of Americans. One in every five youngsters in this nation lives in poverty. For Black and Hispanic children the number is one in every two. Altogether, nearly thirteen million U.S. children lived below the poverty line during 1985. We saw many of them in soup kitchens across the country, standing in line with their parents, brothers, and sisters waiting to get a meal for the day.

Enter, then, the final factor which brought hunger back to this country. As economic hardship increased and as poverty grew astronomically, the federal government instituted the farthest-reaching cutbacks in assistance programs in our nation's history. Instead of helping its citizens get through the hard times, our leaders pulled the support system out from under them. Families who had been living on the economic margins fell through the tattered safety net and landed in the soup kitchens of America.

Beginning in 1981, changes in government programs and eligibility standards resulted in many of the newly poor becoming ineligible for help. Many others had their assistance cut substantially. At the same time, changes in federal tax policies resulted in families with below-poverty-level income having to pay taxes, while more families among the richest ten percent of the nation had to pay little or none. According to the nonpartisan Congressional Budget Office, from 1983 to 1985, families earning over $80,000 per year received an additional $34 billion in tax savings, while families living below poverty lost $23 billion in income.

Two of the most basic food programs—food stamps and school meals—were cut substantially, even as need was increasing so greatly. Funding for these programs was slashed a total of $12 billion over a four-year period. Three million children were knocked from the school lunch program. Some half million were dropped from the school breakfast program. And a total of approximately three thousand schools around the country were forced to close these programs altogether.

Over one million people were cut from food stamps, and all recipients experienced a cutback in benefits. But this was only a part of the story. The food stamp program was designed by Congress to be "countercyclical." When poverty increases, the program should expand to protect more people. So, when poverty rose by nearly six million we would expect food stamp participation to have increased correspondingly. Instead, participation actually dropped. Some ten to fifteen million needy and eligible Americans were not receiving benefits; the problem continues today.

These substantial cuts in federal nutrition programs, coming on the heels of the other factors, caused the return of hunger to America. As need rose, the response of government fell. The cause and the effect are quite clear.

During the 1960s and 1970s, governmental policies virtually brought about an end to hunger; in the 1980s, public policies led to its swift and devastating return. And only governmental policies, we concluded, could again eliminate hunger. Despite the greatest hopes, and much political rhetoric notwithstanding, what we had seen convinced us the private sector is not going to eradicate hunger in our land. We had seen the resources of the churches and social service agencies stretched to the limit. The need is too great and they can do no more.

William Woodside, President of American Can Corporation, put it aptly when he wrote in *Fortune* magazine, "The government created hunger and only the government can solve it." It is ludicrous, Woodside pointed out, for the government to expect industry to do the job. Industry exists to make a profit; government exists to help people.

One of my physician colleagues summed up this concept in medical terms, "This is a government-created epidemic, a man-made disease."

"WE NEED SOMETHING BOLD"

During the spring and summer of 1985, we made numerous trips to Washington to speak with members of Congress and appeared on virtually every major television news program in the country. One of my more memorable experiences occurred with Bryant Gumbel and Jane Pauley on NBC's *Today* show, debating General Robert Leard, a retired military officer appointed by President Reagan to direct the food stamp program.

During the confrontation, Leard denied that hunger was widespread, insisting that "the government has printed millions of brochures to help people get good meals."

"General, people can't eat brochures," I retorted. "They need food."

Our work with members of Congress was much more difficult. Some, like House Speaker Tip O'Neill, were understanding and compassionate. With sad eyes he told us, "You know, when I entered government nearly fifty years ago we thought we were supposed to end problems like this. I wonder if the times have passed us by. I wonder about a nation that lets its children and its seniors go hungry . . . All politics is local," he went on, explaining that the politicians should not forget the people in the "three deckers" in their districts. "No matter how important you feel you may be, their hopes and dreams, their pain and suffering, is behind the doors of those homes. You're supposed to be there to help them when they're down on their luck."

On the Senate side, we had problems. Jesse Helms responded to our report with a vituperative attack, essentially ducking the findings and assailing the Task Force itself. Gordon Harper noted wryly, "I guess the practice of killing the messenger isn't dead after all." As Chairman of the Senate Agriculture Committee, Helms worked hard to protect federal subsidies for tobacco farmers, while railing against nearly every other form of government "welfare." Our report had called for a 25 percent increase in food stamp benefits, an amount that we felt was quite modest compared to the actual need. Helms responded by filing legislation to cut the program by several billion dollars more than it already had been trimmed. His proposal would have been devastating.

We went to see Senate Majority Leader Robert Dole, in the hope that a cooler head might prevail. Dole, however, was unavailable, so we spoke with young staff aide Chris Bolton. With an impatient edge to her voice, Bolton echoed the view espoused earlier by Bill Emerson: "You know the Senator [Dole] believes strongly we have to balance military spending with domestic spending. We can't just throw money at problems." Vic Sidel, an authority on the medical consequences of nuclear war, was angered by this response. "Young lady, I came to talk about hunger but I can also talk about weapons systems," he fired back. "Are you telling me that Mr. Dole wants to build weapons instead of providing more food for the people of this nation? It would be truly ironic, wouldn't it, if in our efforts to defend ourselves against the Russians, we let our own people die of hunger." Unfortunately, we never did get to speak with Dole. As a major supporter of Reagan Administration policy, he clearly was trying to avoid talking about the hunger issue.

Some Republicans, however, were more open-minded. A week after our conversation with Dole's aide, Joyce Lashoff and I met with Senator Mark Andrews, a conservative Republican from North Dakota. As we left our meeting, Andrews was approached by a newsman who thrust a microphone under his chin. Looking earnestly into my eyes he gave credence to our findings. "Dr. Brown, there are now twenty million hungry Americans. This is a serious problem and our nation simply has to respond." Andrews was concerned about the economic depression in the farm industry and hunger in his state. In future months, he would be helpful.

Ted Kennedy, the senior Senator from Massachusetts, traditionally has been sympathetic to the needs of the poor and immediately was responsive to our findings. He also set up a meeting for us with his colleague Ed Zorinsky, who represents the opposite wing of their party. At the meeting, Zorinsky was openly deferential and respectful of Kennedy's intelligence and leadership position. Kennedy told Zorinsky, "These doctors, you know, have been around the country looking at this hunger program and I know of your own concern about it. So, I'm pleased you could take the time to join me to try to figure out what we might do to help them solve it."

Meanwhile, in the House, with its Democratic majority, we found many sympathetic and responsive contacts. Democrats Leon Panetta, Chairman of the Agriculture Subcommittee, and Mickey Leland, Chairman of the House Select Committee on Hunger, championed the issue.

By now the battle lines were well drawn in the Congress and the administration. On one side Helms and the White House proposed legislation to decimate the food stamp program further. In opposition, Panetta and Leland were working to keep current levels of funding. Unfortunately, even with the best of outcomes we would only be treading water. What was desperately needed was an increase in nutrition assistance nationwide; a *minimum of five to seven billion dollars more* in federal appropriations. With anything less, the epidemic would continue to spread.

I asked for a meeting with Panetta and Leland to discuss the issue. "Helms," I said, "is shifting the debate to a choice of doing bad and doing worse. We need you to set out an alternative vision. We need something bold, not just more of the same." To their credit, neither congressman took my suggestion personally, but both were certain about the near impossibility of getting more money out of Congress when the mood of the nation seemed to support selfishness. "People see hunger in their communities," Leland commented, "and Reagan stands up there and says it doesn't exist. People seem to believe him, not what they see themselves." Panetta confided he thought most of his colleagues realized that more should be done, but many were unwilling to stick their necks out. In the end, both men said they would do more. It was a promise each would keep.

After months of hard lobbying Panetta scored a stunning victory, shepherding legislation through the House to increase nutrition programs by five hundred million dollars over five years. While the amount was only a tiny fraction of what was needed, the victory gave us heart. It was possible to take on the White House and win.

In the 1986 session of Congress, Panetta joined with Leland and other House Members, along with Kennedy and several Senate Republicans, in an effort to add a billion more dollars to federal nutrition programs. The tide was turning, although not fast enough.

"HUNGER COUNTY, USA"

During this period, I was approached by leaders of USA for Africa who voiced concerns about the swiftly spreading epidemic of hunger in America. The name of USA for Africa already had spread around the world. From remote villages in South Africa to small towns in Finland, children sang "We Are the World." The record brought in revenues of over fifty millions dollars, most of it going for emergency relief and development assistance in Ethiopia and sub-Saharan Africa.

Approximately ten percent of the proceeds from their internationally acclaimed hit had been targeted for domestic purposes. Now, the artists wanted to learn more about hunger in the United States. Marty Rogol, the Director of USA for Africa, and Irwin Redlener, a physician in charge of their medical committee, asked me to help plan their efforts in the United States. I was appointed as a member of the medical task force and chairman of the committee on hunger in America.

On several occasions I flew to California to meet with celebrities I previously had seen only on television or in the movies: Kenny Rogers, Lionel Richie, Michael Jackson, Karen Black, Edie Adams, Robert Goulet, Terry Moore. It was enormously gratifying to learn of their genuine concern for America's hungry and homeless. I described what we had learned about the problem, and the artists deliberated on the direction their efforts should take. One group felt that all funds raised should go for programs providing direct aid to the hungry; others felt that public education was vitally necessary.

I pointed out that even if the artists could raise fifty million dollars—the amount they collected for Africa—it would feed the hungry for only three days. I reiterated the conclusion we had drawn from our field investigations: private giving was important, but it would not solve the problem. In the final analysis, the government would have to do the lion's share of the work.

Ken Kragen, the Hollywood manager who had masterminded USA for Africa, suggested the idea of a large community event that would raise money *and* consciousness. "Hands Across America" thus began as a simple concept, but with an unprecedented scope. Ordinary citizens would form a human chain from one end of the nation to the other. The event would provide money for direct aid to programs feeding the hungry as well as raise public awareness.

At the kickoff press conference, my remarks were sandwiched between those of Ken Kragen and the president of Coca-Cola, a major sponsor for the event. Some weeks later, I met Kenny Rogers at a Los Angeles press conference introducing the "Hands Across America" theme song. The singer leaned over to introduce himself, saying he had seen me on television and admired my work. Returning the compliment I whispered in his ear, "Kenny, I've been on nearly every major television program in the country and, thankfully, my son is unaffected by it all. But, what would really impress him would be your autograph." Rogers laughed and took a few minutes to write Alex a note which he signed, "Your friend, Kenny."

At the press conference, the artists explained their involvement. Rogers, for instance, said, "Larry, I grew up on welfare. While I can't say I remember ever going hungry, I know that we often had little to eat. I don't want other people to go through what I did."

USA for Africa had a specific mission for the Physician Task Force. Why, they asked, did the federal food stamp program not reach more people? If our nation has such a program, and if it once nearly wiped out hunger, why was it not working now? USA for Africa provided a grant to Harvard to send us back into the field to see what was wrong with the food stamp program.

THE WHITE HOUSE ATTACKS

Because food stamp eligibility is closely tied to poverty, we first identified counties across the nation where more than 20 percent of the residents live below the poverty line. Then, we selected those counties on the list where fewer than one-third of the poor were receiving food stamp benefits. We termed these areas "Hunger Counties" and targeted them for our next field investigations.

In all there were 150 such counties around the country. Far fewer than we anticipated were in the south; many were in the Midwest. Apparently threatened by our analysis, many state and local officials in the targeted states reacted with criticism and denials.

Release of the hunger county data analysis hit the media in a bigger way than our work the year before. The press conference announcing our upcoming fieldwork was carried on all the television networks. I was asked to come to Washington for a live interview on *The MacNeil/Lehrer* show, appearing with Reagan Administration spokesman Assistant Secretary of Agriculture John Bode. Bode, a former Jesse Helms aide, cited statistics on food stamp participation that contradicted data his own agency previously had supplied to Congress. He volleyed a number of broadsides at me personally and used the platform the show provided to mouth platitudes about the administration's record.

Bode's barrage was to be the beginning of an orchestrated effort to discredit our work. Within a week he wrote a letter to Harvard President Derek Bok, charging that I was bringing disrespect to the University. (I later learned he wrote to another college president, attempting to have a professor who disagreed with him publicly fired.) Two weeks after the *MacNeil/Lehrer* interview, Lawrence Cranberg, identifying himself as General Secretary of "Accuracy in Media," attempted to disrupt a public meeting of the Physician Task Force in Austin, Texas. He also wrote a letter to Derek Bok, using many of the same charges and language that Bode had used. It was clear that the two worked together, in a curious marriage between a right-wing organization attempting to influence academic research and a supposedly nonpartisan government official.

Several days after, I received a death threat. It probably was unrelated to these events, but it was chilling just the same. Late one afternoon, my staff took a call for me from a man in Montana. "You tell that Harvard doctor," the voice warned, "that I heard he was coming. I got my rifle polished and waiting for him."

Meanwhile, Congressman Bill Emerson joined in Bode's efforts, telling the press he had asked the Government Accounting Office (GAO) to investigate our analysis for potential flaws. A heavy-handed attempt to discredit our work was obviously afoot.

Emerson specifically asked the GAO to determine whether the hunger counties we identified were, in fact, the hungriest places in America. I wrote to him explaining that many other areas of the nation had substantial hunger. Our analysis was designed purely to measure poverty against food stamp participation, as an index of the effectiveness of food stamp coverage. The GAO report subsequently confirmed this point: the "Hunger Counties" did not necessarily judge where the most hungry people in America were living, but provided an indication of the gap between those receiving benefits and those eligible.

After release of the GAO report Mickey Leland issued a

statement, charging that some of his House colleagues seemed more interested in debating methodology than ending hunger. I invited Emerson to travel with us in his own state, so that he could see for himself the dimensions of the hunger problem. I was disappointed when he declined to do so.

During the winter months of 1986 we traveled to hunger counties in Texas, Arkansas, Missouri, South Dakota, Iowa, Georgia, and Florida. We interviewed local government officials, food stamp administrators, recipients, and applicants. This time we did not make house calls or visit soup kitchens and food pantries. We knew hunger existed. Our task was to learn why the food stamp program, once so successful, was no longer doing its job. We wanted to establish why just over half the poor were getting food stamps. When asked by the press about our new mission I would draw an analogy everyone could relate to: "How would you feel if the IRS returned only half the refund checks owed to taxpayers and you didn't get yours?"

"Worse Than IRS Forms"

In 1981 the federal government initiated sweeping changes in the food stamp program. The President had promised it would be better targeted to serve the "truly needy." Fewer people might be eligible for assistance, but more of the hungry would be helped. That promise went unfulfilled. In 1980, 68 percent of the poor were receiving food stamps; by 1985 the number tumbled to 59 percent. Just on the basis of the statistics, there seemed to be a contradiction between the President's promise and reality.

As we did our fieldwork it seemed that about half the people we met hated us, the other half loved us; hardly anyone seemed indifferent. Many local officials were angered by our investigation, maintaining that there was no hunger in their area or being embarrassed by having it pointed out. Prior to our arrival in Brazos, Texas, for example, County Administrator Judge Holmgreen told the press that we were "wacko" and our figures "were screwy." He said we erroneously had included Texas A & M students in our calculation of the county's poor, although we had not done so. We scheduled a meeting with him to clear the air.

Before the meeting, I stopped by the county food stamp office to speak with the administrator. According to our data, only 12 percent of the eligible poor in Brazos County were receiving food stamps. The local food stamp office calculated the participation rate at about 14 percent, prompting food stamp official Erwin Dabbs to say, "We agree with the Harvard numbers."

We arrived at Holmgreen's office and found reporters waiting for the meeting. I began the interview by saying I was sorry if we had caused distress, but that I thought our data was accurate. I added that the food stamp office had confirmed our numbers. The Judge thanked me for coming and took time to talk about the county. But he never disputed the data. The press had a field day. The *Houston Chronicle* treated the meeting like the shoot-out at the OK Corral: "The Eastern Varmint came into town and told Brazos officials exactly what he had told the nation: the county has a hunger problem."

Holmgreen's hostile reaction to our work was hardly unique. A food stamp official in Missouri called our analysis "stupid," and his counterpart in South Dakota accused us of having a political agenda for our work. On the other hand, some food stamp officials, like Chris Murphree, whom we had met in Greenwood, Mississippi, were deeply concerned about the bureaucratic red tape and regulations preventing needy people from obtaining benefits.

We found the food stamp officials who were most angered by our presence were worried about politically sensitive matters in their own states. Following our visit to Missouri, for example, the food stamp director was forced to resign his post for awarding state contracts to a private group headed by his wife. In South Dakota, the official who attacked us was in the middle of a primary campaign battle between the governor and a U.S. senator. The controversy raised by our work thrust him into the political fishbowl.

"THE IDEOLOGUES ARE WINNING"

Ironically, our very first meeting with Erwin Dabbs in Brazos County, Texas, set the tone for what we would learn in 1986. Not only were the computer statistics truly revealing, but there were readily identifiable reasons for the relatively small percentage of poor people receiving food stamps. Pointing to a pile of seven manuals stacked on a table, Dabbs said, "There are some one hundred policy changes that have been handed down in the last four years that keep us in constant turmoil. On top of this the federal government penalizes the state if we do not run at 95 percent accuracy. The constant changes in the complicated rules make this difficult, if not impossible. As a result, program operations frequently come to a halt."

In Florida, state official Bill Hanson gave his impression: "Federal officials are trying to reduce food stamp services, not through Congress but by administrative decree. The ideologues are winning." Iowa's human services director, Larry Jackson, labeled the federal regulations as "complicated . . . just crazy. If fans stopped coming to NFL football games something would be wrong with the rules of the game. The food stamp rules need to be changed to let the needy people participate." A welfare official in Mississippi said, "Why, you ask, do two hundred and eight thousand Mississippians eligible for food stamps not get them? The answer is the hassle." The head of the program in Illinois said people had to be "Olympic pole vaulters" to get over the paperwork and red tape.

In Arkansas, Commissioner Walt Patterson said, "The federal rules are *intended* to set up barriers to keep eligible people from getting food stamps. The barriers are mindboggling . . . and they work." And in Florida, Josephine Colston, director of the state's program, said, "If you set up a process where it takes thirty days to get help when you're hungry, if you make verification procedures tedious enough, and if you skew the program by threatening the states with fiscal sanctions, people will drop out of the system. If you can go through the food stamp process, you can go through anything."

President Reagan was, in fact, correct about one thing. Many poor people do not ever apply for food stamps because they are unaware of the program or do not know how to obtain benefits. A variety of studies demonstrate that one-third to one-half of eligible people who fail to get assistance cite lack of information about the program as the reason. In reviewing these studies, the General Accounting Office reported that "no other factor had the sweeping impact on non-participation as did poor information concerning eligibility status." Yet knowing this, the Reagan Administration had Congress terminate funds for food stamp outreach, prohibiting the states from using federal funds to locate needy people. Monies could not be used for radio announcements or newspaper ads, not even to tell people where to apply for benefits. As a result, nearly every state in the nation canceled outreach and education activities.

Many people, we found, also have difficulties getting to the food stamp offices. Most counties have only one office, so potential applicants often must travel twenty or thirty miles to apply. A number of counties we visited are between one thousand and three thousand square miles. Being poor, by definition, makes it unlikely that one will have a car, certainly not a new and reliable one. Moreover, public transportation in rural areas is virtually nonexistent. In Texas, for example, the adjoining towns of Bryant and College Stations are ten miles in length, yet neither town has public transportation. In Baca County, Colorado, an elderly woman who runs out of food during the winter has the almost impossible task of getting to the food stamp office ten miles away, through winter snows on back roads.

In Missouri, food stamp worker Rosanna Bradshaw told us, "If someone happens to leave one paper at home we will not be able to certify them. That means they will have to go back ten or twenty miles to the house, return the same distance back to our office and then return home again . . . all of this expense and effort and sometimes they get only twenty dollars in food stamps. It makes no sense."

Again and again we heard that sheer physical distances and the fact that no public efforts were being made to overcome this obvious problem were preventing the hungry from getting food stamps. Other government agencies, such as social security, permit people to apply and receive benefits by mail. Yet, USDA regulations not only prohibit application by mail, but in many localities require monthly benefit re-certification to be performed at the food stamp office.

We found also that large numbers of poor people were being terminated from the food stamp program despite the fact they are obviously eligible. In Beaufort County, North Carolina, for instance, 85 percent of people cut from the program are eligible; in Dewey, South Dakota, the number is 75 percent; in Franklin, Florida, 70 percent; in Pulaski, Georgia, 68 percent. The pattern is too consistent and obvious not to be deliberate in design. Martha Carroll, director of the Arkansas Hunger Project, minced no words about this. "Middleclass America would not tolerate the bureaucratic system imposed on the poor in the food stamp program if they knew about it or if it was imposed upon them."

Before becoming a physician, my colleague George Pickett ran the welfare department in California. To illustrate the complexity of the forms, George gave legislators blank food stamp applications to complete. Usually he found the lawmakers unable to fill them out correctly. George describes the food stamp application forms as "more onerous than the IRS tax forms." Many highly educated persons have an accountant file their tax returns, yet with much ballyhooing publicity the Reagan Administration recently championed legislation to simplify tax reporting. It is completely unreasonable to expect the poor, many of whom do not have advanced education, to properly fill out paperwork that is too complicated for our lawmakers.

In North Carolina, for example, we found a semiliterate mother who, upon arrival at the food stamp office, was given eleven forms to complete and a list of income and employment documents. Unable to understand and complete them, she asked her minister for assistance. He was unable to wade through the paperwork, so she returned to the office to ask for help. She was denied food stamps because she had not complied with the verification process.

We also found otherwise eligible persons terminated from the food stamp program due to unrealistic asset requirements. In each case, these people had no money to buy food. In Cambden, Arkansas, for example, we found fifty-eight-year-old Jean Lucas who applied for food stamps two months after finding out she had cancer. While her limited income made her eligible for food stamps, the assessed value of her two-year-old car made her ineligible. However, she needed the car to get to the hospital for chemotherapy treatments. Malcolm Johnson applied for food stamps after losing his Missouri farm in a foreclosure proceeding. He took all available income and financial records to the food stamp office only to learn his request for assistance was denied because he was unable to prove he had no income.

Tom Travis, a Texas father, became unemployed when his plant closed. He reluctantly applied for food stamps after watching his children go without food, but was told he would have to get a social security number for the youngsters. His eldest child was two years old. When Tom went to get social security numbers for the children, he was told to produce birth certificates. The process took nine weeks while the family had little to eat.

In Missouri, we followed Ada White through the application process. Because there is no public transportation in her area, she had to pay seven dollars for a ride to the food stamp office fourteen miles away, where she picked up the application forms. She was given the forms to complete and return by mail, along with many things to do: verify social security income, medical bills, account for medication expenses, rent, and utility bills. She was told to return to the food stamp office in two weeks.

Due to illness, Ms. White was unable to make her appointment and called to reschedule. She was told she could not be seen for another two weeks. On the day of her new appointment, she paid another seven dollars for transportation only to be told that some of the forms had not been filled out correctly. She could have been ruled ineligible because of these errors, but the individual food stamp worker was sympathetic and helped her correct the mistakes. Nevertheless, Ms. White needed another rent receipt. The food stamp worker apologetically said the federal requirement could not be overlooked. Her case was postponed until the rent receipt could be obtained and mailed to the food stamp office.

A little more than one week later, Ms. White's case was approved. She received an authorization form, which meant she could obtain food stamps—in another two weeks. By the time she received her food stamps nearly two months had transpired. She was awarded a ten-dollar monthly benefit for her endurance.

In 1984, President Reagan's own hunger task force faulted such bureaucratic impediments in the food stamp program. Pointing to their onerousness, they gave examples: "The determination of net income incorporates a formula with five deductions . . . determination of eligibility requires ten mathematical computations . . . [and] the application form and requisite worksheet cover nine pages of detailed questions." The group recommended streamlining this cumbersome process, but the White House opposed doing so at every possible turn.

New rules also have led to an adversarial relationship between the federal and state programs that ultimately translates into a reduction in the number of eligible people receiving benefits. Chief among the rules is mandatory monthly reporting, which requires recipients to complete a new set of forms each month, whether or not they have new income. Because the reporting is tedious and errors are likely, both clients and program administrators resent the process. The client feels the worker is being unreasonable and the worker feels the client is not being cooperative. A combative relationship is formed.

Federal auditors also come to the states to review food stamp files. If all of the pertinent forms are not at least 95 percent accurate, the federal government may impose stiff penalties. This forces local food stamp officials to be extremely rigid in applying rules and ultimately becomes the reason for denying benefits when there is *any* doubt about the information supplied on the onerous forms.

"We have a gun to our heads. We operate under a fiscal sanction system, not a social service system," one food stamp worker explained. "We're between a rock and a hard place," agreed a Missouri food stamp worker. "For five years the feds have done nothing but complicate the process. We're at just under a six percent error rate now; if they sanction us we'll lose staff and be even worse off. For several years the only concern has been the error rate, not helping people. It hurts the whole program."

The conclusion from our fieldwork, corroborated by numerous studies, is that the federal requirements purportedly designed to reduce state errors have made it *more likely* that mistakes will be made. A 1985 GAO study, for instance, found that the states attribute many of their errors to unnecessary and cumbersome federally mandated paperwork.

There is only one reason, said Arkansas Commissioner

Walt Patterson, for the maze of regulations: "To reduce eligibility and set up barriers to participation in the food stamp program." "The purpose of the food stamp program used to be to raise nutritional levels," observed an official in Texas, "now it's to keep poor people from coming on the program. The federal government is trying to harass the states in order to kill the program."

From the very beginning of the Reagan Administration the food stamp program was targeted for deep cutbacks. In 1981 Robert Carlson, former welfare director under Reagan in California, was summoned to Washington. Carlson already had demonstrated his ability to reduce the number of people receiving public assistance in California, where he increased the paperwork load, required monthly re-certification, and placed inordinate burdens on clients and government bureaucrats. He was asked to put a similar system in place on the federal level for the food stamp program.

In July 1984, *The Wall Street Journal* ran a front-page story documenting the elaborate maze of forms and procedures that had produced the termination of thousands of needy families from the food stamp rolls. Carlson retorted, "All recipients have to do is fill out a simple little form."

And whatever the operating philosophy, the truth is that the vast majority of food stamp households do not contain people who could or should be working. Sixty-two percent of recipients are children; many others are elderly or disabled. Nearly all fall below the federal poverty level. Many have incomes so low that even if they were doubled, the family would still live below the poverty line. Most recipients receive benefits for only a short period of time, and then only about a dollar and fifty cents per family, per meal.

Much public ballyhoo was also made over alleged waste, fraud, and abuse in the food stamp program, allegations never supported by federal study and definitely not confirmed in our investigations. It was deeply disturbing to all of us that a family's breadwinner could be terminated from the program because he was unable to produce a twenty-dollar receipt for cleaning a parking lot, while front-page stories carried reports of massive waste, fraud, and abuse in defense spending. In the David and Goliath battle between the nation's poor and the Department of Defense for federal dollars, David seldom wins. What was incomprehensible to us was the pro-Goliath attitude of so many politicians.

We presented our findings on the reasons for hunger counties to the public, Congress, and, of course, to the Board of USA for Africa in May of 1986 in a report, "Increasing Hunger and Declining Help: Barriers to Participation in the Food Stamp Program." Despite clear evidence that poverty had increased in our land, relatively fewer Americans were receiving help from the government. Something was dreadfully wrong. We called it the "Hunger Gap."

Our findings led to heated public debate. My colleagues and I appeared on television, and our findings were carried widely in the print media. Representatives from the White House and Department of Agriculture openly challenged the validity of our findings.

We did not know then, but the President himself would later step out to challenge us directly.

"Hands Across America"

The night our study hit the network news, public interest in hunger was peaking in anticipation of "Hands Across America," scheduled for May 25, 1986. Would enough people actually show up to form a human chain, six million strong, across an entire continent? Would the President join us, despite his repeated denials that hunger exists? The White House already had announced that Mr. Reagan would not participate in the event, although many speculated that his refusal would be politically disastrous.

Following coverage of our report on hunger at the top of the news hour, the networks went directly to on-going preparations for "Hands Across America." Later we learned that Reagan and a Midwestern high school boy were watching these broadcasts at the same time, albeit miles apart. The next day the student and his classmates were guests of the President at a previously scheduled visit to the White House. During the question-and-answer period, the boy asked Mr. Reagan why the nation spends so much money on destructive weapons and foreign aid when it does not feed many of its own people. In this simple manner, the young student echoed the substance of Vic Sidel's statement to Robert Dole's staff aide.

The boy's remark prompted the President to respond with an assertion that there is plenty of food in America, but "the hungry are too ignorant to know where to get it." The telephone at my office started ringing about ten minutes after the President finished speaking: first the Associated Press, then the *Baltimore Sun*, then CBS News and *The Washington Post*. I daresay no one believed the President. While newspapers carried my response to the President's extraordinary gaffe, Ted Kennedy's response went to its heart. "The ignorance," he said, "is in the White House."

Days later, I flew with my fiancée and son to Washington to participate in "Hands Across America." Marty Rogol and Kenny Rogers had asked that I represent USA for Africa in the nation's capitol. We stood amidst a crowd outside the gates of the White House and watched as the President and Mrs. Reagan held the hands of the staff in a line across the lawn. Whether one agrees or disagrees with President Reagan's policies, one cannot deny that he is quick to join the winning side of an issue—even if it takes help from an anonymous high school boy from the Midwest.

7

A Disease America Can Cure

OUR THREE YEARS of investigations had, by now, placed the issue of hunger high on the national agenda. The President himself had been forced into the discussion, despite his repeated efforts to downplay the problem. His appearance at "Hands Across America" seemed to signify that the national conscience could no longer be easily ignored.

Clearly, our work alone had not turned the tide. National religious groups had conducted their own studies, and anti-hunger organizations, like the Food Research and Action Center, worked tirelessly to keep hunger in the public eye. The Children's Defense Fund saw to it that Congress would come to terms with the growing impoverishment of youngsters. And in my mind, few matched the effectiveness with which Bob Greenstein and his colleagues at the Center on Budget and Policy Priorities in Washington would get the attention of leaders on Capitol Hill.

By the winter of 1985 our collective efforts had turned the debate around, preventing further cutbacks in nutrition programs for the poor. When Jesse Helms and other ultra-conservatives tied to the administration spewed ugly diatribes on the floor of Congress, few listened. We even had been successful in getting five hundred million dollars added to the food stamp budget. While this figure still fell woefully short of the actual need, it was a major victory at a time when the administration was looking for additional cuts in social spending, even while asking for more in military appropriations.

What truly matters, of course, is our success at ending hunger in our nation. By this measure, I am sorry to say, our efforts have fallen far short of the intended goal. The available data point to the disheartening conclusion that poor and working-class families are sinking further into the abyss of poverty. Millions of Americans are going hungry on a regular basis, while too little help is coming from government. Too many Americans are still unaware of the hunger epidemic and the job of educating them is still unfinished.

"THE DISEASE OF MALNUTRITION"

What it all comes down to is food. Food is required by the body to carry out all of its vital functions. It supplies the raw materials necessary for building and replacing tissues, the energy for work and play, and the nutrients to drive the chemical processes that support life itself.

To the medical professional, hunger is a symptom, not a disease. In its mildest form it is an uncomfortable craving; over longer periods it becomes a torturous physiological experience that affects all of the other senses.

Malnutrition, on the other hand, is a *disease* that occurs when the body is deprived of vital nutrients over an extended period of time. Without the right food, provided at the right time, no organism will function properly. Deprive a fetus or infant of adequate nutrition, and its brain will not develop normally. Withhold food from a growing child and its body will quickly waste; over a longer period the youngster will be permanently stunted in growth.

Malnourished people of all ages are susceptible to many illnesses. They are especially prone to anemia, intestinal and skeletal disorders, and infections. In the early stages of malnutrition the face appears deceptively young. In the later stages the visage becomes almost expressionless, old, and withered. The pupils react sluggishly when stimulated by light; the skin loses its normal resilience and becomes dry and pale; the hair thins, adding to the withered appearance.

In advanced malnutrition the hands and feet lack warmth and color; the muscles weaken, the subcutaneous fat wastes away. Both children and adults take on a puffy look; in very advanced cases the abdomen and extremities swell noticeably. These are signs of advanced protein deficiency, called "kwashiorkor," such as we see in African famine photographs. As the condition exacerbates, the body becomes unable to maintain normal temperature, blood pressure, and pulse rate; heartbeats become faint. Diarrhea, generally accompanied by bleeding from the intestines, appears. Women stop menstruating, men become impotent; both adults and children lose the ability to control urination. Sores appear that do not heal; bones break but do not mend.

Severe malnutrition devastates the nervous system. The reflexes become flat and sluggish, the mind loses its ability to reason. The individual withdraws, eventually sinking into a fetal position. Only food stimulates the psyche, so that the withdrawn individual may suddenly become aggressive if food is sensed. When the disease is far advanced, however, even interest in food is lost. There is no energy to struggle.

Prolonged malnutrition thus affects virtually every organ and tissue in the body. In the state known as "marasmus" the body devours its own tissues; the internal organs atrophy, leaving only the brain at its customary weight. The cause of death, more often than not, is overwhelming infection occurring when the immune system fails.

Tragically, as we traveled around the country, we verified reports of Americans suffering from severe malnutrition: children diagnosed with kwashiorkor, marasmus, or cavitary tuberculosis; adults and children literally dying from starvation, suffering severe wasting or contracting serious infectious diseases.

Malnutrition, of course, is not an absolute disease state, but a continuum in which an individual may be mildly, moderately, or severely affected. The kind of malnutrition we see most commonly in the United States is called "silent undernutrition" by the World Health Organization. As the term implies, it usually goes unnoticed. Like a car whose fuel has been watered down, silently malnourished people operate far below optimal performance levels. Eventually, the gasoline may be so watered that the engine no longer runs. When this occurs, one passes from the state of silent undernutrition to frank malnutrition. In its early stages the undernourished system can be rejuvenated with proper treatment; when the condition is advanced, irreversible injury or death results.

The victim of silent undernutrition in America is the baby born seriously underweight, whose disease makes it forty times more likely than a normal child to die before the age of one. It is also the three-year-old whose clothing hides the fact his weight is several pounds below the bottom of normal range on the growth charts. Or it may be the youngster who is docile, apathetic, and withdrawn at school, who does not learn and play because her body lacks sufficient fuel.

The victim of silent undernutrition is the senior citizen whose clothing falsely conveys a sense of health, when a sign proclaiming that person "Frail and Emaciated" would be far more accurate. It is the woman who falls and fractures her hip because her bones are weak and brittle. It is also the "skin-and-bones" man who appears at the hospital emergency ward with a reactivated case of tuberculosis years after successful treatment; the drugs do not fail, but malnutrition insidiously destroys his immune system.

Malnutrition is a pernicious destroyer of intellect. The human brain grows rapidly from conception until almost the age of two years, attaining approximately 80 percent of its full development. If adequate nutrients are not provided during this "window of opportunity," brain weight and size will be irreversibly compromised. The result is the child who never reaches his intellectual potential, who will be mildly to moderately retarded for an entire lifetime.

This is the picture of hunger in America today. Less dramatic, perhaps, than in Africa, but no less real. It is easy to miss, even for physicians. Many of our doctors were schooled during better times, when silent undernutrition was virtually unknown on our hospital wards. The trained practitioner, however, knows this disease, just as the observant parent knows a child is sick long before others detect signs of a problem.

"HUNGER IS KILLING OUR NATION'S POOR"

Hunger is, of course, no more than a barometer of poverty. Inadequate income, probably more than any other single factor, determines the amount of hunger and nutrition-related illness in our nation.

If we treat public health as an equation where x plus y yields z, we can say that sufficient income plus the good nutrition it buys yields good health. Today, most families living at or below the poverty line cannot purchase even a minimally adequate diet to see them through normal times. When they unexpectedly face a new stress, such as an illness, their already meager resources become truly inadequate.

In order to evaluate nutrition, the medical profession uses standards adopted by the National Academy of Sciences that define an adequate diet in terms of recommended dietary allowances (RDA's). The RDA's present the case for normal, healthy people; they can be adjusted upwards to account for special needs such as pregnancy, breastfeeding, and chronic illnesses. Recent studies indicate that even in "normal times" America's poor cannot afford to purchase a diet that meets the RDA's. The situation inevitably becomes aggravated at times when more than the RDA's are required, so that pregnant women and growing children, as well as seniors with chronic diseases, are at exceptionally high risk for malnutrition.

In Massachusetts, clinical evidence of malnutrition among children first emerged in the spring of 1982. It was further documented in 1983 in a statewide survey of children seeking medical care at public health clinics in poor communities. Researchers found that over ten percent of the children were below the fifth percentile for height, a sign of stunted growth, and over 12 percent showed at least one indicator of under-nutrition. Children living in poverty were found to be twice as likely to suffer stunted growth as those living above poverty.

Research in Ohio, Minnesota, and Illinois has corroborated the findings in Massachusetts. A study of predominantly poor children seen at Cook County Hospital revealed that 21 percent of the youngsters were below the tenth percentile for height. The National Nutrition Surveillance Survey of four hundred thousand children conducted in thirty-two states by the Centers for Disease Control found approximately eight-and-a-half percent of children under the age of six stunted in growth, with seven percent suffering from anemia. Applying these rates nationally suggests that half a million American children under age six are suffering from malnutrition. These figures may represent only the tip of the iceberg.

While health professionals understand the significance of these statistical data, lay people may be confused. Following testimony I presented to the Senate Agriculture Committee on the subject of growth failure, I found myself challenged by Jesse Helms.

"How can you conclude that finding fifteen percent of poor children at the bottom of the growth charts really represents a serious problem?" Helms asked.

"The charts are designed so that only five percent of any random pediatric population will be at the bottom fifth percentile for growth measurements," I responded. "There is nothing normal about the failure of poor children to grow."

Perhaps he understood all along, but did not wish to hear the grim truth. Among scientists, however, finding 15 percent of children retarded in their normal growth and development is a sign for *grave* concern. Until proven otherwise, the underlying cause is most likely to be malnutrition.

The infant mortality rate (IMR) is another highly sensitive measure of nutritional status, as well as one of the best general indicators of public health. The rate represents the number of babies who die before the age of one for every thousand live births. Because it is computed annually, it serves as an excellent barometer of recent changes in public health conditions. IMR is important because it is available for the areas covered by census studies, census tracts, thus permitting public health experts to compare the health status of people in relatively small communities. The infant mortality rate is also important because it is computed in the same manner throughout the world. Comparing our IMR to other nations provides an invaluable tool with which to assess public health in the United States against that of other countries.

Compared to other nations, we do not do very well in guaranteeing the lives of our newborns. Currently, seventeen other nations, including virtually all of Western Europe and Japan, have lower infant mortality rates than the United States. And in recent years our record has been getting worse. In 1976 we ranked twelfth; in 1980 we were sixteenth; by 1983 we had fallen to eighteenth.

Moreover, while the IMR for affluent Americans was decreasing, the IMR for many poor Americans was *increasing*. In some of the poorest counties we visited, the IMR was at levels seen only in impoverished Third World nations. During the early years of this decade, when economic conditions were at their lowest ebb and the government was turning a cold shoulder to the poor, the infant mortality rate actually increased in eleven states. If we look only at black births, the rate went up in thirteen states. Today, black infant mortality is more than double that for whites nationally.

While scientists expect some slight state-to-state or community-to-community fluctuation each year, the IMR differences we find cannot be dismissed as insignificant. One cannot justify, for instance, that the IMR in New York's affluent Sunset Park section of Brooklyn is 5.8, while in nearby Brownsville it is 25.3. Or that the IMR is 7.5 on Manhattan's Upper East Side while in Central Harlem it is 25.6.

These examples are not unique to New York City. While the nation's overall infant mortality rate is approximately 10.9, rates as high as 60 can be found in the census tracts of certain cities and with rates higher than 30 in some rural counties. In Hale County, Alabama, for instance, the infant mortality rate is 31. The infant mortality rate for blacks in our nation's capitol exceeds that of some of this hemisphere's poorest nations—such as Panama, Guyana, Tobago, Cuba, and Jamaica.

It is telling that infant mortality rates in the United States are invariably inversely proportional to income. The lowest rates are found in our wealthiest communities; the highest IMR's are always seen in our poorest communities. While the link between poverty, hunger, and ill-health appears to be irrefutable generally, the infant mortality rate is one of the most shocking indictments of our government's policies toward the poor.

There is an irony to these statistics. Millions of public dollars are being spent on sophisticated technology to save babies born ill or inadequately developed, even as we have cut back in important programs for the poor. Today, hospital care for these "high-risk" infants averages up to $167,000 per child, an astronomical figure in comparison to the cost of proper nutrition and prenatal care that can help prevent these tragic births.

Infant mortality is, of course, only the worst possible health outcome of inadequate nutrition and poverty. Infant mortality is associated with low birth weight (LBW), defined as a weight of less than 2,500 grams (about five-and-a-half pounds) at birth. So serious is LBW that it is the eighth-leading cause of death in our nation; an LBW child is so frail that it is forty times more likely to die than a baby born within the normal range for weight. Today over six percent of all babies born in America have low birth weight, giving this nation the unenviable record for having the worst birth-weight distribution of any industrialized nation in the world.

Like infant mortality, LBW is related to household income: the poorer the family, the greater the likelihood of an LBW delivery. In many communities the LBW situation has gotten worse, not better, in recent years. Just prior to our field visit, a study at Nashville General Hospital found that the number of low birth weight deliveries had increased. Not surprisingly, we also found that 34 percent of the patients reported running out of food by the end of the month and that the poverty rate had increased substantially in the community.

While it is easier to diagnose nutrition problems in children, there is no doubt that adults also are the victims of silent undernutrition. Several factors determine the dietary needs of the elderly, including disease, heredity, general level of activity. Eighty-five percent of the people over retirement age suffer from at least one chronic disease that influences what they need to eat. Some of these ailments, like mild hypertension, are quite common and require only modest dietary changes (like lowering salt intake). Other diseases, such as diabetes, require more precise diet control. A third category of conditions, like osteoporosis, is directly related to metabolic changes in late adulthood that require careful intake of nutrients. Moreover, as people age the basic metabolic rate diminishes, so the demand for nutrient-dense foods increases. Usually this means eating a high-quality diet that is relatively expensive to purchase.

The opportunity for any elderly American to enjoy a prolonged lifespan is directly related to diet. Unfortunately for many seniors, particularly the millions on fixed incomes, nutrient-rich foods like fresh vegetables, quality meat, and dairy products are expensive. It should be no surprise, therefore, that low-income adults are at increased risk of suffering nutrition-related disorders, a pattern reflected in the disproportionate rate of certain diseases. Black Americans, a major low-income group, are 1.47 times more likely to suffer from cardiovascular disease, 1.37 times at greater risk for pneumonia and influenza, and 2.21 times more likely to suffer diabetes than white Americans who, on the whole, are not so impoverished.

A survey conducted in Tulsa, Oklahoma, found that the city's elderly poor consumed only 77 percent of the RDA's for calories, 89 percent for protein, and 86 percent for calcium. A study conducted by the Texas Department on Aging and the Senate Interim Committee on Hunger and Nutrition discovered that 34 percent of elderly participants would go hungry without community-sponsored feeding programs. Fifty-eight percent said the subsidized food was their only complete meal of the day. These observations, however, are not unique to the elderly poor of Oklahoma or Texas.

Although we do not have a precise count of the adult Americans adversely affected by hunger, it would be prudent to heed the words of my colleague Irwin Rosenberg, Director of the Clinical Nutrition Research Center at the University of Chicago. In testimony before Congress, this former President of the American Society for Clinical Nutrition urged that our leaders address hunger aggressively and decisively: "We have enough information at hand to conclude that hunger is killing our nation's poor."

"THE BIGGEST LIE"

Approximately fifty million Americans fall below the poverty line at some time during a given year, while more than thirty-three million are impoverished over any twelve-month period. The disparity between rich and poor is greater in the United States than all but one other industrialized nation. No other developed country has so many poor people or treats them as badly as we do.

Besides its devastating effects on the body, hunger is destructive to the family and the very fabric of American life. We heard this message, for example, in Massachusetts from Mr. Abruzzi, who said, "If I cannot provide for my children, then I feel inept as a parent and ashamed." Later, we listened as an unemployed factory foreman in Chicago shook his head in dismay and told us, "I'm seeing women and children scavenging from garbage cans." We heard it in St. Louis, where a father broke down in tears as he described abandoning his wife and children so they could qualify for public assistance.

Being hungry in a wealthy nation ultimately undermines confidence in our government. Again and again we heard the poor cry out in rage, "Our leaders don't care." They bear the scars of the mean-spirited rhetoric of some of our top leaders.

Each year since taking office in 1981, the Reagan Administration has proposed additional budget cuts in programs for the poor. In June 1986, after he had succeeded in slashing twelve billion dollars from food stamp and school meals programs, President Reagan said his administration was "spending more on nutrition than has ever been spent before . . ." This statement was smoke and mirrors. It ignored both the increased number of people who had fallen into poverty and the rise in the cost of living.

At that same press conference, the President reported ". . . the federal government is providing, I think, ninety-three million meals a day . . ." In fact, for a large majority of those meals the government was paying only a small fraction. For example, the President was counting sixty million meals a day for twenty million food stamp recipients. But any poor person listening knew all too well that forty-nine cents was not buying them a meal.

At another press conference, Mr. Reagan looked into the television cameras and in his most persuasive voice told the American public, "If one child in this land is hungry, that is one child too many." Yet, at that very moment he was asking Congress for additional cuts in federally sponsored nutrition programs. Shortly thereafter the nation was to hear the President declare, "I find it difficult to find any cases of starvation and undernourishment."

One can only feel rage at Assistant Secretary of Agriculture John Bode, who went on national television in 1986 with blatantly false figures to cover government cuts in nutrition programs. Only months later Bode suppressed the results of a prominent commission, sponsored by his own Department, that had found the WIC program to be an effective means of reducing low birth weight. Fearful that Congress would appropriate additional funds to expand WIC, Bode held onto the results for a year. Finally, he altered the findings and released them on a Friday before a holiday, hoping to squelch press coverage.

And there were Edwin Meese's comments that hunger is "anecdotal" and that "people are in soup lines because the food is free." Suffice it to say that we found Meese's words had no bearing in reality. We must also consider the Democrats and Republicans in Congress who moved in lock-step behind the President, happy to ride on his political coattails even when they disagreed with his policies. Their bipartisan silence permitted the administration to point an accusatory finger and decry "waste, fraud, and abuse" at social programs, while the Defense Department was paying over nine thousand dollars for a twelve-cent wrench and more than a thousand dollars for a plastic stool cap worth about thirty-four cents.

The combination of rhetoric and mindless acquiescence led to hunger and malnutrition—and to blaming the victims for a disease the government created.

ERADICATING AN EPIDEMIC

After more than three years of trying to comprehend how there could be so much hunger in such a rich land, we finally had found the answer. We had discovered an epidemic born out of political ideology and government policy; a man-made disease caused by leaders who, rather than falling asleep on watch, stood firmly at the helm and purposely dismantled programs that had been successful at preventing widespread hunger in our nation for years.

On the positive side, we should remind ouselves that what has been done by the hand of man can be undone. The programs that once were successful in eliminating hunger are still in place. We need only re-fund them to the levels we know will do the job.

The social policies that created hunger in America are the results of political trade-offs and domestic priorities. Beginning at the end of the Carter Administration and escalating enormously during the Reagan years, the federal government put in place policies that transferred billions of dollars from poor to rich. An ill-conceived tax package gave billions to certain Americans while creating unprecedented federal deficits. And, of course, there was the costly military build-up the likes of which had never before been seen in peacetime America. My colleague Victor Sidel points out, "If one had spent a million dollars a day from the moment Christ was born until today, it would still not equal half the amount the Reagan Administration has appropriated for military spending."

While acknowledging the importance of a strong national defense, one must question whether all of this incredible spending has been the most cost-effective means for securing our national security. One B-1 Bomber, for example, costs approximately four hundred million dollars and will last about four years. That amount of money would provide school lunches for a quarter-million hungry children for a decade. Two CVN nuclear attack carriers cost over seven billion dollars. That amount, used to strengthen existing nutrition programs, would virtually eradicate hunger in America.

In his June 1986 press conference President Reagan said, ". . . we thought it [food stamp outreach] was a waste, that they [food stamp recipients] would rather buy more food stamps." Yet, the truth was that none of the five million dollars saved annually by eliminating food stamps was ever used to put more food on the table for poor people. The same legislative act that terminated food stamp outreach also cut food stamp benefits by over one billion dollars.

Perhaps we should ask ourselves not *whether* we have permitted such rhetoric to cloud our vision, but *why*. Surely we must begin again to help raise people out of poverty by investing in their future.

Hunger in the United States is a man-made disease that can be cured. The disease was created quickly, but we can eradicate it even more quickly. It is a question of national conscience—and will.

INDEX